BON APPÉTIT®

Light & Easy

Desserts

VOLUME TWO

BON APPETIT PUBLISHING CORP.
PUBLISHER

LOS ANGELES

Light & Easy

INTRODUCTION

When talk turns to dessert, the words "light" and "easy" don't automatically spring to mind. But this book dazzlingly proves that desserts can indeed be easy to make as well as light on both the palate and—in a good many cases—the waistline.

Taken from the pages of recent issues of *Bon Appétit* magazine, the recipes that follow encompass a tempting array of sweet treats: from fresh and cooked fruit desserts to satisfying puddings and ethereal mousses; homebaked cakes to golden-brown pies, pastries and tarts; refreshing frozen desserts to simple, crisp cookies. They all share an incomparable ease of preparation, with a significant number taking only a few minutes of actual work apart from baking or freezing times. All of them also reflect our modern taste for fresh, clean flavors in the dishes we cook

and eat. And many of the recipes have been created with today's dietary needs in mind—reducing the fat and calories without sacrificing an iota of satisfaction.

Throughout the book, you'll also find an intriguing selection of special guidelines, tips and hints to inspire your own dessert creations and provide you with a taste of the latest information on healthy contemporary cooking.

Used together with its companion volume—which covers the rest of the meal from appetizers through entrees to side dishes—this book aims to bring you the very best of contemporary cooking as it is captured month after month in *Bon Appétit*. Enjoy these recipes as they help you make your cooking lighter and easier than ever before.

BON APPÉTIT®

Light & Easy Desserts

VOLUME TWO

CONTENTS

continued on next page

Fruit Desserts

A platter of ripe seasonal fruits makes the simplest, lightest dessert of all. But, as the recipes on the following pages demonstrate—from Strawberries with Cassis to Baked Peaches with Cointreau; from Pears Poached in Red Wine to Fresh Citrus Compote; from Raspberry and Fig Gratin to Grand Fruit Salad—it is indeed possible to embellish upon nature's own handiwork to delightfully appetizing effect.

PEACHES AND RASPBERRIES IN SPICED WHITE WINE

8 SERVINGS

1 bottle (750 ml) Italian dry white wine, such as Pinot Bianco or Pinot Grigio
½ cup sugar
4 ¾x2-inch orange peel strips (orange part only)
3 cinnamon sticks
6 peaches
2 ½-pint baskets raspberries
Biscotti

Combine 1 cup wine, sugar, orange peel and cinnamon in small saucepan. Stir over low heat until sugar dissolves. Increase heat; simmer 15 minutes. Remove from heat; add remaining wine.

Blanch peaches in large pot of boiling water 20 seconds. Transfer to bowl of cold water using slotted spoon. Drain. Pull off skin with small sharp knife. Slice peaches and transfer to large bowl. Add raspberries and wine mixture. Cover and refrigerate at least 1 hour (*Can be prepared 6 hours ahead. Stir occasionally.*) Divide fruit and wine among glass goblets. Serve with biscotti.

STRAWBERRIES WITH CASSIS

20 SERVINGS

6 1-pint baskets strawberries, hulled and halved or quartered (depending on size of berries)
1¼ cups crème de cassis liqueur
⅓ cup sugar
2 tablespoons fresh lemon juice
3 cups chilled whipping cream
3 tablespoons powdered sugar

Combine first 4 ingredients in large bowl. Let stand at room temperature 1 hour, stirring occasionally. (*Can be prepared 3 hours ahead. Refrigerate.*)

Whip cream and powdered sugar in large bowl until stiff peaks form. Spoon ⅔ cup berries and some juices into each of 20 balloon glasses. Top each with spoonful of whipped cream and serve.

MEDLEY OF FRESH NECTARINES, BLUEBERRIES AND PLUMS

Summer fruits cooked with a little sugar and topped with sweetened sour cream are a simple, delectable dessert. Pass shortbread or sugar cookies, if desired.

6 SERVINGS

6 large ripe nectarines, pitted, each cut into 6 wedges
2 1-pint baskets blueberries
⅔ cup sugar
12 purple plums, pitted, quartered
Lightly sweetened sour cream
Fresh mint leaves

Mix nectarines, blueberries and sugar in heavy large saucepan. Cook over medium heat until nectarines are just tender, stirring occasionally, about 5 minutes. Transfer to bowl. Cool completely;

Mix in plums. Cover and refrigerate until well chilled. (*Fruit mixture can be prepared 6 hours ahead.*)

Spoon fruit into bowls. Top with dollop of sour cream. Garnish with mint and serve immediately.

STRAWBERRIES WITH CUSTARD SAUCE

The sauce can be served warm or cold.

4 SERVINGS

2 cups whole or lowfat milk
¼ cup sugar
2 tablespoons cornstarch
2 egg yolks
1 tablespoon brandy
1 teaspoon vanilla extract
2 1-pint baskets strawberries, hulled
Ground cinnamon
4 fresh mint sprigs

Whisk milk, sugar, cornstarch and yolks in heavy medium saucepan until smooth. Cook over medium-high heat until mixture boils and thickens, whisking constantly, about 3 minutes. Remove from heat. Mix in brandy and vanilla. (*Custard can be prepared 1 day ahead. Transfer to bowl. Press plastic wrap onto surface and refrigerate. Whisk in additional milk to thin custard if desired before serving.*)

Divide berries among 4 glass bowls. Spoon custard over. Sprinkle with cinnamon. Garnish with mint and serve.

BERRIES KIR ROYALE

2 SERVINGS

2 cups halved strawberries
1 tablespoon sugar
½ cup chilled champagne or sparkling wine
1 tablespoon crème de cassis

Mix strawberries and sugar in medium bowl. Let stand 5 minutes, stirring occasionally. Divide between 2 large wineglasses. Pour ¼ cup champagne and ½ tablespoon cassis into each glass.

BAKED PEACHES WITH COINTREAU

6 SERVINGS

⅓ cup peach nectar
6 peaches, peeled, halved, pitted
3 tablespoons brown sugar
⅓ cup Cointreau or other orange liqueur
3 tablespoons chilled unsalted butter, cut into small pieces
Vanilla frozen yogurt
Additional Cointreau or other orange liqueur (optional)

Preheat oven to 375°F. Generously butter 9-inch square baking dish. Pour nectar into prepared dish. Arrange peaches cut side up in dish. Sprinkle with sugar. Drizzle Cointreau over. Top with butter. Bake until peaches are tender, about 30 minutes. Let cool 10 minutes.

Scoop frozen yogurt into bowls. Top with peaches; spoon juices from dish over. Serve, passing additional Cointreau separately if desired.

Fruitful Suggestions

High in fiber and vitamins, fresh fruit is a must for any well-balanced diet. And its natural sweetness makes fruit the perfect healthful snack or dessert.

To benefit from extra vitamins and fiber, eat or prepare washed fruit with the peel intact whenever possible.

Use puréed fresh or frozen fruits, such as berries and apricots, for naturally sweet yet low-cal dessert sauces.

To add sweetness and flavor to cereals and plain yogurt, try fresh or dried fruit instead of processed sugar.

For a simple and quick jam that can be very low in added sugar: Cook diced fruit in a small amount of water, covered, until tender. Sprinkle sugar to taste and continue to cook, uncovered, until thick. Store in refrigerator.

Raw grated apple adds moisture to meat loaf without adding fat.

Cook diced fruit—bananas, apples, pears or apricots—with hot breakfast cereal to provide sweetness and texture without adding processed sugar.

Purée frozen banana pieces with yogurt or lowfat milk and vanilla extract for a nutritious, rich-tasting "shake."

Fruit juice concentrates can be substituted for sugar in some recipes. Use apple juice concentrate in place of sugar to sweeten iced tea or yogurt.

Toss diced bananas, apricots or melon with fresh lime juice and perhaps a dash of cayenne pepper or ground cumin for a speedy chutney that has no added salt or processed sugar.

Cantaloupe, papaya and large peach or nectarine halves make delicious "bowls" for chicken or seafood salads.

POACHED PEACHES
WITH VANILLA

A sophisticated dessert that is great on its own, mixed with sweet berries or used as a topping for frozen yogurt.

4 SERVINGS

1 cup semisweet white wine (such as French Colombard)

½ cup water

⅓ cup sugar

2 tablespoons honey

1 vanilla bean, split lengthwise

1¼ pounds firm ripe peaches (unpeeled), cut into ½-inch-thick slices

Bring first 5 ingredients to simmer in heavy medium saucepan, stirring to dissolve sugar Remove from heat. Scrape seeds from vanilla bean into syrup. Return bean to syrup. Cover and continue simmering 5 minutes. Add peaches and poach until just tender when pierced with tip of sharp knife, about 4 minutes.

Transfer mixture to bowl and refrigerate until cold, at least 3 hours. (*Can be prepared 3 days ahead.*)

Remove vanilla bean and any loose pieces of peach skin before serving.

LOWFAT FROMAGE

DELICATE, CREAMY AND, BEST OF ALL, low in fat, *fromage blanc* is the perfect accompaniment to fresh fruit at breakfast or after dinner. This fresh (uncured and unripened) white cheese is made from cow's milk that is drained and left in unsalted curds. Similar to cottage cheese, fromage blanc is available stateside either plain or with fruit. Look for it in specialty foods stores and some supermarkets.

HONEY-POACHED APRICOTS
WITH STAR ANISE

The combination of star anise, fresh ginger and vanilla bean adds an exotic nuance to this refreshing dessert.

4 SERVINGS

1 pound firm ripe apricots

3 cups water

½ cup honey

1 4x½-inch strip lemon peel (yellow part only)

1 tablespoon fresh lemon juice

3 ⅛-inch-thick slices fresh ginger

1 star anise*

½ vanilla bean, split lengthwise

Vanilla yogurt

Fresh mint

Cut apricots in half. Discard pits. Combine 3 cups water, honey, lemon peel, fresh lemon juice, fresh ginger slices and star anise in heavy medium saucepan. Scrape seeds from vanilla bean into pan;

add bean. Bring to simmer over high heat, stirring to dissolve honey. Add apricots. Reduce heat to low and simmer until apricots are tender, about 7 minutes. Using slotted spoon, transfer apricots to medium bowl.

Increase heat to high and boil until syrup is reduced to ⅔ cup, about 30 minutes. Strain syrup over apricots. Cool to lukewarm. Cover and refrigerate. (Can be prepared 1 day ahead.)

Spoon apricots into shallow bowls. Spoon some syrup over Top with dollop of yogurt. Garnish with fresh mint.

*A brown, star-shaped pod. The anise "rays" each hold a seed. Available at Asian markets and specialty foods stores.

BAKED PINEAPPLE WITH BROWN SUGAR AND KAHLÚA

2 SERVINGS
CAN BE DOUBLED OR TRIPLED

½ small pineapple, peeled, cored, cut lengthwise into ½-inch-thick spears
3 tablespoons brown sugar
1½ tablespoons butter
¼ teaspoon cinnamon
3 tablespoons Kahlúa or other coffee liqueur

Vanilla ice cream

Preheat oven to 400°F. Arrange pineapple in single layer in baking dish. Sprinkle with brown sugar. Dot with butter and sprinkle with cinnamon. Drizzle Kahlúa over. Bake until pineapple juices bubble, 25 minutes.

If necessary, transfer juices to small saucepan and boil until thickened to sauce consistency. Arrange pineapple on plates. Top with ice cream. Spoon sauce over and serve hot.

MOROCCAN ORANGE SALAD

A refreshing dessert.

6 SERVINGS

6 large navel oranges, peeled, white pith removed
1 tablespoon orange flower water* (optional)
1 tablespoon powdered sugar
¾ teaspoon ground cinnamon
Sliced almonds, toasted
Fresh mint leaves

Cut oranges into thin rounds. Arrange orange slices in concentric circles on serving platter. Sprinkle with 1 tablespoon orange flower water if desired. (Can be prepared 1 hour ahead. Cover and refrigerate.) Combine sugar and ground cinnamon and sprinkle over orange slices. Sprinkle with toasted almonds. Garnish orange slices with fresh mint leaves and serve.

*A flavoring extract available at liquor stores and in the liquor or specialty foods section of supermarkets.

STRAWBERRY-ORANGE SHORTCAKE

An oversize shortcake for a wonderful summer dessert or afternoon teatime sweet. The biscuit is split in half, filled with berries and served with a strawberry sauce. As a flavor boost, beat a few tablespoons of your favorite orange liqueur into the whipping cream if desired.

6 SERVINGS

STRAWBERRY SAUCE

1 1-pint basket strawberries, hulled, halved
⅓ cup sugar
2 tablespoons orange juice

BISCUIT

2 tablespoons warm water (105°F to 115°F)
1 envelope dry yeast
Generous pinch of sugar
2½ cups all-purpose flour
⅓ cup plus 1 tablespoon sugar
1 tablespoon grated orange peel
2 teaspoons baking powder
2 teaspoons baking soda
½ teaspoon salt
½ cup (1 stick) chilled unsalted butter; cut into pieces
1 cup sour cream

BERRIES

2 1-pint baskets strawberries, hulled, sliced
⅓ cup sugar

1 cup chilled whipping cream, lightly sweetened, whipped

FOR SAUCE: Stir hulled strawberries, sugar and orange juice in heavy large non-aluminum saucepan over medium heat until sugar dissolves. Boil 1 minute. Cool slightly. Coarsely puree berry mixture in processor using on/off turns. Cover and refrigerate until well chilled. (*Can be prepared 2 days ahead.*)

FOR BISCUIT: Line cookie sheet with parchment. Lightly flour parchment. Place 2 tablespoons warm water in small bowl. Sprinkle yeast and pinch of sugar over; stir to dissolve yeast. Let stand until foamy, about 5 minutes.

Blend flour, ⅓ cup sugar, orange peel, baking powder, baking soda and salt in processor. Add butter and cut in until mixture resembles coarse meal. Using on/off turns, blend in sour cream, then yeast mixture. Turn dough out onto lightly floured surface and knead just until smooth, about 15 seconds.

Transfer dough to prepared cookie sheet. Press dough into 9-inch round. Sprinkle with remaining 1 tablespoon sugar. Cover loosely and let rise in warm, draft-free area 30 minutes.

FOR BERRIES: Toss sliced berries with ⅓ cup sugar in medium bowl. Cover and refrigerate at least 30 minutes and up to 3 hours.

Preheat oven to 375°F. Bake biscuit until top is golden brown and beginning to crack, about 20 minutes. Transfer to rack and cool.

Using serrated knife, carefully cut warm or room-temperature biscuit horizontally in half. Place bottom half of biscuit on platter. Cover with ⅔ of sliced strawberries. Slide top half of biscuit over. Spoon remaining sliced strawberries over. Cut shortcake into wedges. Transfer to plates. Serve with strawberry sauce and whipped cream.

RASPBERRY AND FIG GRATIN

4 SERVINGS

2 baskets fresh raspberries
6 fresh figs, quartered
8 ounces sour cream

½ cup firmly packed dark brown sugar
Mint sprigs

Preheat broiler. Arrange raspberries and figs in 10-inch-diameter broilerproof baking dish. Stir sour cream until smooth; spoon evenly over fruit. Sprinkle with brown sugar. Broil close to heat source until brown sugar melts and bubbles, about 4 minutes. Garnish with mint and serve warm.

BROILED PINEAPPLE WITH COCONUT AND BROWN SUGAR

Good-tasting things don't get much simpler than this super-speedy dessert. It's delicious on its own or served with big scoops of your favorite ice cream.

2 SERVINGS
CAN BE DOUBLED

1½ tablespoons unsalted butter, melted

4 ½-inch-thick peeled fresh pineapple slices
2 tablespoons brown sugar
1½ tablespoons flaked or shredded sweetened coconut

Preheat broiler. Brush some butter over bottom of 8x8-inch broilerproof baking dish with 2-inch-high sides. Arrange pineapple slices in dish. Sprinkle brown sugar over. Drizzle remaining butter over. Broil pineapple about 4 inches from heat source until topping is golden brown and bubbling, about 2 minutes. Sprinkle coconut evenly over pineapple slices. Broil until coconut is toasted, about 30 seconds.

Pears Poached in Red Wine

A recipe that's a year-round delight. In summer, when peaches are in season, they can be used instead of pears to create this light and sophisticated dessert.

8 SERVINGS

3 cups dry red wine
1 cup sugar
1 cinnamon stick, broken into 4 pieces
½ vanilla bean or 2 tablespoons vanilla
4 whole cloves
4 firm ripe pears, peeled

Bring red wine, sugar, cinnamon, vanilla and whole cloves to boil in heavy large saucepan. Add pears and simmer until tender but not mushy, turning occasionally, about 15 minutes. Transfer pears and syrup to large bowl. Refrigerate until well chilled, about 4 hours. (*Can be prepared 2 days ahead.*)

Cut pears lengthwise in half and remove cores. Starting ½ inch from stem end, make several lengthwise cuts in each pear half. Transfer pear halves to plates. Press gently on pears to fan slices. Serve pears with syrup.

Summer Fizz

SELTZERS AND SPARKLING MINERAL waters are great warm-weather coolers—but while you're sipping, are calories sneaking up on you? Although a variety of flavored sparklers are calorie-free, many are not, according to the *University of California at Berkeley Wellness Letter.* The publishers say to watch out for those beverages with added sweeteners that can increase calorie counts to match those of regular colas. Look for drinks labeled "calorie-free" or, better still, "calorie- and salt-free."

Peach-Honey Smoothie

2 SERVINGS

1¼ cups plain lowfat yogurt
1 pound ripe peaches, peeled, pitted, sliced
2 tablespoons fresh lemon juice
¼ cup honey
¼ teaspoon vanilla extract

Divide 1 cup yogurt among 8 sections of ice cube tray. Freeze until yogurt cubes are solid, at least 4 hours. (*Can be prepared 1 day ahead; keep frozen.*)

Puree peaches with lemon juice in processor or blender. Add remaining ¼ cup yogurt, honey and vanilla. Process until mixture is well blended. Add frozen yogurt cubes and process until mixture is smooth and frothy. Pour into chilled tall glasses and serve.

HANDY FRUIT SNACK

FREEZING WINTER WEATHER USUALLY means slim pickings in your grocery store's fruit department. But dried figs from California's San Joaquin Valley are plentiful year-round. Loaded with nutrients—they contain 80 percent more potassium than bananas do and are full of calcium—this fruit is cholesterol-free, virtually sodium- and fat-free and is perfect with cereals and rice dishes or in muffins. Dried figs are also extremely high in dietary fiber. (If you're counting calories, though, measure carefully: There are 220 in a half-cup serving.) For recipes and additional information, send a business-size SASE to the California Fig Advisory Board, Dept. BA, P.O. Box 709, Fresno, CA 93712.

FRESH CITRUS COMPOTE

Try over frozen yogurt, ice cream, pound cake, or serve with your favorite cookies.

8 SERVINGS

SYRUP

2 cups sweet orange muscat wine (such as Essensia)
1 cup fresh orange juice
¼ cup sugar
1 star anise*
½ vanilla bean, split lengthwise

FRUIT

3 oranges
1 pink grapefruit
3 kiwi, peeled
¼ pineapple, cored, peeled

Vanilla frozen yogurt or ice cream

FOR SYRUP: Bring all ingredients to boil in heavy medium saucepan. Boil until liquid is reduced to ¾ cup, about 25 minutes. Using small sharp knife, scrape vanilla seeds into syrup; return bean to syrup. Cool. (Can be made 1 day ahead. Cover and store at room temperature.)

FOR FRUIT: Cut peel and white pith off oranges and grapefruit. Using small sharp knife, cut between membranes of oranges and grapefruit to release segments. Cut each kiwi into 8 wedges. Cut pineapple into ½-inch-thick slices. Drain fruit. Place in bowl. Discard vanilla bean and star anise from syrup. Pour syrup over fruit and stir to combine. Serve over vanilla frozen yogurt or ice cream.

A brown, star-shaped pod. Each "ray" holds a seed. Available at Asian markets and specialty foods stores.

GRAND FRUIT SALAD

Here's a lovely light dessert and a colorful and delicious addition to a brunch menu.

8 SERVINGS

2 cups green grapes
2 cups sliced strawberries
2 cups sliced plums

1 cup sliced peaches
1 cup orange segments
1 cup sliced peeled kiwi
½ cup Grand Marnier or other
   orange liqueur
½ cup orange juice
2 tablespoons sugar

Plain yogurt or sour cream
Ground cinnamon

Combine all ingredients in large bowl. Cover and refrigerate up to 8 hours.

Combine all ingredients except yogurt and ground cinnamon in heavy medium saucepan. Bring to boil, stirring until sugar dissolves. Reduce heat and simmer until fruit softens, stirring occasionally, about 20 minutes. Transfer fruit only to glass bowl, using slotted spoon. Boil liquid until reduced to 1 cup, returning liquid exuded from fruit to saucepan, about 10 minutes. Pour liquid over fruit, discarding orange slices. Serve warm, room temperature or chilled, topping with yogurt and cinnamon.

DRIED FRUIT STEWED WITH BROWN SUGAR AND VANILLA

This fruit keeps for several days in the refrigerator and is delicious for breakfast, too. Any dried fruit works well

4 SERVINGS
CAN BE DOUBLED OR TRIPLED

4 cups water
½ cup firmly packed brown sugar
1 8-ounce package mixed dried fruit
4 orange slices
1 cinnamon stick
1 1½-inch piece vanilla bean, split
   lengthwise

SUMMER FRUIT COMPOTE WITH BOURBON AND MINT

Almost any variety of colorful summer fruit works well in this compote.

6 TO 8 SERVINGS

SYRUP

1 cup water

½ cup sugar
¾ cup chopped fresh mint (about
   2 large bunches)
¼ cup bourbon
1 tablespoon fresh lemon juice

COMPOTE

½ large honeydew melon, seeded
8 ounces dark sweet cherries, pitted
3 nectarines, thinly sliced
3 tablespoons thinly sliced fresh
   mint
Fresh mint sprigs

FOR SYRUP: Stir 1 cup water and sugar in heavy medium saucepan over low heat until sugar dissolves. Add chopped fresh mint. Boil over medium heat 5 minutes. Cool completely. Strain into small bowl, pressing firmly on mint. Mix bourbon and lemon juice into syrup. (*Can be prepared 3 days ahead. Cover and refrigerate.*)

FOR COMPOTE: Scoop honeydew with melon baller. Combine melon balls, pitted cherries, sliced nectarines and sliced fresh mint in large bowl. Add syrup and toss thoroughly to combine. Refrigerate compote at least 20 minutes and up to 2 hours.

Garnish compote with mint sprigs.

FRESH FRUIT WITH TRIPLE SEC AND RUM

24 SERVINGS

9 oranges

1 cup triple sec or other orange liqueur

½ cup sugar

6 tablespoons rum

3 pineapples, peeled, cored, cut into bite-size pieces

3 1-pint baskets fresh blueberries or 6 cups seedless grapes

3 1-pint baskets strawberries, hulled

1 cup toasted slivered almonds (optional)

Cut peel and white pith from oranges. Using small sharp knife, cut between membranes to release orange segments. Cover and refrigerate until ready to use. *(Can be prepared 6 hours ahead.)*

Combine triple sec, sugar and rum in large bowl. Stir until sugar dissolves. Add pineapple and toss to coat. Cover and refrigerate 3 to 6 hours.

Add orange segments, blueberries and strawberries to pineapple and toss gently. Mound fruit on platter or in large bowl. Sprinkle with toasted slivered almonds if desired and serve.

RHUBARB AND PEAR COMPOTE

Any extras are great cold for breakfast. As an alternative to the vanilla ice cream, top with sour cream or lowfat yogurt for a lighter interpretation.

2 SERVINGS

CAN BE DOUBLED OR TRIPLED

¼ cup dry red wine

¼ cup plus 2 tablespoons sugar

¼ teaspoon ground allspice

2 Bartlett pears, peeled, cut lengthwise into eighths, cored and cut crosswise into 1-inch pieces

10 ounces rhubarb, trimmed, cut into 1-inch pieces

Vanilla ice cream

Bring first 3 ingredients to simmer in heavy medium saucepan over medium-low heat, stirring until sugar dissolves. Add pears and simmer 2 minutes. Mix in rhubarb. Cover and simmer until rhubarb and pears are just tender, stirring occasionally, about 8 minutes. Spoon warm compote into bowls. Top with ice cream and serve.

Fresh Summer Fruit with Granola Topping

This quick, unbaked fruit "crisp" is made by sprinkling a crunchy, low-fat granola over sliced seasonal fresh fruits.

4 SERVINGS

GRANOLA

2 cups old-fashioned or quick-cooking oats
¾ cup sliced almonds
½ cup raisins
¼ cup honey
1 tablespoon vegetable oil
½ teaspoon ground cinnamon

FRUIT

2 nectarines, pitted, sliced
2 plums, pitted, sliced
½ 1-pint basket strawberries, hulled
½ ½-pint basket blueberries
3 tablespoons orange juice

FOR GRANOLA: Preheat oven to 350°F. Combine oats, sliced almonds and raisins in 13x9-inch baking pan. Bring honey, vegetable oil and cinnamon to boil in heavy small saucepan, stirring mixture constantly. Pour over oat mixture and stir until evenly distributed. Bake granola until golden, stirring frequently, about 18 minutes. Cool in pan. Crumble granola into pieces. Store airtight at room temperature. (*Can be prepared 2 weeks ahead.*)

FOR FRUIT: Toss nectarines, plums, strawberries, blueberries and orange juice in medium bowl. Let stand 20 minutes at room temperature.

Divide fruit among dishes. Sprinkle each serving with ¼ cup granola.

Focus on Quality

"WHEN WE THINK ABOUT HEALTHFUL eating habits, we usually focus on the amount of fat in the dishes we make rather than the quality of the ingredients. We forget to think about where produce is grown, how long it's been stored or how it traveled to our markets. Whenever it's possible, buy organically grown fruits and vegetables in season from local farmers. When the produce is fresh, naturally ripened and consumed quickly, there's really no need to enhance it. It's the best way to eat, simply and healthfully."

Alice Waters
**Owner: Chez Panisse, Café Fanny;
Berkeley, California**

Puddings & Mousses

You can make a little bit of something rich go a long way, as the recipes that follow deliciously demonstrate. In Orange Caramel Flan, for example, regular and evaporated milk stretch three eggs into six satisfying servings. Air whisked into egg whites lifts a White Chocolate and Orange Soufflé to ethereal heights. These, and the other recipes that follow, amount to nothing less than culinary legerdemain.

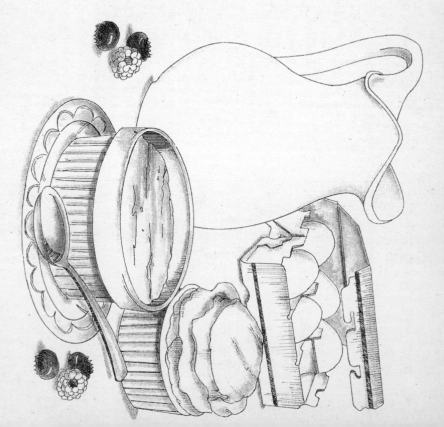

BLUEBERRY PARFAIT TRIFLES WITH LEMON ZABAGLIONE

Individual trifles are stunning and luscious.

MAKES 6

BLUEBERRY SAUCE

2½ cups fresh blueberries
¾ cup sugar
¼ cup fresh lemon juice

ZABAGLIONE

6 large egg yolks
¾ cup sugar
1 cup champagne, sparkling wine or sauternes
2 tablespoons fresh lemon juice
2 teaspoons grated lemon peel
1 cup chilled whipping cream

1 1-pint basket (about) blueberries
6 ounces amaretti* crumbled
Fresh mint sprigs

FOR SAUCE: Coarsely puree berries in processor. Transfer berry puree to heavy medium nonaluminum saucepan. Add sugar and lemon juice and bring to boil, stirring frequently. Reduce heat and simmer until thickened, about 3 minutes. Pour into bowl. Cover and chill until cold. (*Can be prepared 2 days ahead.*)

FOR ZABAGLIONE: Whisk yolks and sugar in medium metal bowl to blend. Set bowl over saucepan of simmering water and whisk until foamy, about 5 minutes. Add champagne, lemon juice and lemon peel and whisk until mixture triples in volume and candy thermometer registers 160°F, about 4 minutes. Remove from over water. Let stand until cool, whisking occasionally, about 30 minutes. Cover and refrigerate until well chilled. (*Can be prepared 1 day ahead. Keep refrigerated.*) Beat whipping cream to medium-stiff peaks in large bowl. Fold whipped cream into zabaglione.

Spoon 1 tablespoon blueberry sauce into each of 6 balloon-shaped wineglasses or dessert goblets. Top each with spoonful of fresh blueberries. Top each with ¼ cup zabaglione. Sprinkle each with 1½ tablespoons crumbled cookies. Repeat layering twice. Cover and refrigerate desserts and remaining zabaglione at least 3 hours and up to 8 hours. Top each dessert with spoonful of zabaglione. Sprinkle with crumbled cookies and more berries. Garnish with mint springs.

*Italian macaroons available at Italian markets and some supermarkets.

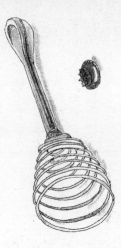

DOUBLE BERRY PUDDING

Based on an English recipe, this cold summer pudding is traditionally made with stale bread. This version uses purchased angel food cake instead. It takes about 20 minutes to make and should be prepared at least one day ahead.

4 SERVINGS

1 purchased angel food cake, cut into ⅓-inch-thick slices, crusts trimmed

3 cups fresh blackberries or frozen unsweetened, thawed

1 cup sugar

3 cups fresh raspberries or frozen unsweetened, thawed

¾ cup chilled whipping cream, lightly sweetened, whipped

Butter 6-cup soufflé dish. Slightly overlap enough cake slices to cover bottom and sides of prepared dish, pressing cake gently against sides to adhere.

Cook blackberries and ½ cup sugar in heavy medium saucepan over medium-high heat until sugar dissolves and berries release their juices, stirring gently, about 2 minutes. Spoon berry mixture into cake-lined dish. Add raspberries and remaining ½ cup sugar to same saucepan. Cook over medium-high heat until sugar dissolves and berries release their juices, stirring gently, about 2 minutes. Spoon raspberry mixture over blackberry mixture. Cover with remaining cake slices. Cover top of dish with waxed paper. Set plate atop dessert; weight with heavy object. Refrigerate at least 24 and up to 48 hours.

Remove weight, plate and waxed paper from pudding. Turn pudding out onto plate. Serve with whipped cream.

ORANGE CARAMEL FLAN

Make this satisfying dessert a day ahead so it can firm up in the refrigerator. With fewer eggs than usual and no whipping cream, it is lighter than most flans.

6 SERVINGS
215 CALORIES PER SERVING

½ cup sugar
1 tablespoon water
3 large eggs
¼ cup frozen orange juice concentrate, thawed
1 12-ounce can evaporated milk
½ cup milk (do not use lowfat or nonfat milk)
2 teaspoons vanilla extract
⅛ teaspoon almond extract

Orange slices
Mint leaves

Preheat oven to 300°F. Mix ¼ cup sugar with water in heavy small saucepan. Cook over medium-low heat until sugar dissolves, stirring frequently. Increase heat and boil without stirring until sugar turns deep golden brown, swirling pan occasionally. Immediately pour caramel into six 6-ounce custard cups. Carefully tilt cups slightly, covering as much of bottoms (not sides) as possible. Set cups aside.

Whisk eggs, orange juice concentrate and remaining ¼ cup sugar in large bowl. Gradually whisk in both milks and extracts. Divide custard among prepared cups. Place cups in large baking pan. Add enough hot water to pan to come halfway up sides of cups. Bake until custards are set, about 1 hour 20 minutes. Remove cups from water. Cover and refrigerate overnight. (*Can be prepared 2 days ahead.*)

Run small sharp knife around custard sides to loosen. Invert 1 custard onto each plate. Garnish with orange slices and mint leaves and serve.

WHITE CHOCOLATE AND ORANGE SOUFFLÉ

This moist orange-flavored soufflé is rich with white chocolate. Offer snifters of orange liqueur to sip alongside.

6 SERVINGS

½ cup whipping cream
¼ cup sugar
6 ounces imported white chocolate (such as Lindt), coarsely chopped
4 large egg yolks, room temperature
2 teaspoons grated orange peel
2 tablespoons Grand Marnier or other orange liqueur

3 large egg whites, room temperature
Pinch of cream of tartar
2 tablespoons sugar
2 ounces imported white chocolate (such as Lindt), coarsely chopped
Powdered sugar

Preheat oven to 350°F. Butter 6-cup soufflé dish. Sprinkle dish with sugar; tap out excess. Heat cream and ¼ cup sugar in heavy medium saucepan over medium heat, stirring until sugar dissolves. Add 6 ounces of chocolate and stir until chocolate dissolves. Whisk in yolks and orange peel. Cook until mixture thickens slightly, stirring constantly, about 5 minutes; do not boil. Whisk in Grand Marnier. Transfer mixture to large bowl.

Using electric mixer, beat egg whites and cream of tartar in large bowl until soft peaks form. Add 2 tablespoons sugar and beat until stiff peaks form. Mix 2 ounces chopped chocolate into warm egg yolk mixture. Fold in egg whites in 2 additions. Transfer mixture to prepared soufflé dish. Bake until soufflé is puffed and top is golden brown, about 35 minutes. Dust with powdered sugar and serve.

Straight Talk on Eggs

CHANGE IN CHOLESTEROL

According to a 1988 study done by the USDA with the Egg Nutrition Center, the average large egg contains only 213 mg cholesterol, not 274 mg. as was previously thought. That's 22 percent less cholesterol.

FACTS ON FAT

We also know now that a large egg contains five grams of fat— 1.5 grams of which is saturated, 1.9 grams monounsaturated and 0.7 grams polyunsaturated.

THE LAST WORD

Eggs aren't all the dietary villain they've been made out to be. They are nature's most compact form of protein, and are rich in vitamins A, B$_{12}$ and D, calcium, iron and other minerals. It's interesting to note that three egg yolks a week are allowed even in cholesterol-lowering diets. And egg whites, the leanest protein available, have no cholesterol and barely any fat.

SALMONELLA SENSE

The U.S. Department of Agriculture recently decided to establish a program to control the spread of salmonella in table-egg poultry flocks in the United States. The agency is attacking the bacteria on two fronts: They test and certify flocks, and they track the flocks implicated in human cases of salmonella.

And Cathy McCharen of the Egg Nutrition Center in Washington, D.C., has some excellent advice with regard to salmonella. "Any raw animal product contains bacteria. People at high risk for gastrointestinal disturbances, especially the elderly, the very young or the immuno-compromised, should not eat raw eggs, seafood or meat. I still eat Caesar salads, but only in places I know and trust. Proper food handling, refrigeration and sanitation are still the best safeguards against illness."

Frozen Anisette Soufflé

8 SERVINGS

1 cup sugar
⅓ cup water

6 egg whites
6 tablespoons anisette or other anise liqueur
2 cups chilled whipping cream
Fresh fruit such as sliced strawberries, blueberries or raspberries (optional)

Cook sugar and water in heavy medium saucepan over medium heat, stirring until sugar dissolves. Boil *without* stirring until candy thermometer registers 240°F, about 12 minutes.

Meanwhile, with electric mixer beat egg whites in large bowl until stiff but not dry. Beat hot syrup into egg whites in slow steady stream. Mix in 3 tablespoons anisette. Continue beating until mixture is stiff and shiny. Whip cream and remaining 3 tablespoons anisette in medium bowl until peaks form. Fold into whites. Transfer to 8-cup soufflé dish or eight 1-cup ramekins. Cover and freeze until firm, about 8 hours. (*Can be prepared 2 days ahead.*) Garnish with fruit if desired.

Rum 'n Ting Soufflés

Ting is a grapefruit-flavored soft drink popular in Jamaica. When it's combined with rum it makes a refreshing cocktail called "Rum 'n Ting." These soufflés capture the flavor of that libation.

6 SERVINGS

CANDIED PEEL

1 large, thick-skinned pink grapefruit
4 cups water

¾ cup sugar
¼ cup water
2 tablespoons dark rum

SOUFFLÉS

Nonstick vegetable oil spray

¼ cup cold water
¼ cup dark rum
1 envelope unflavored gelatin
4 large eggs, separated
¾ cup unsweetened frozen grapefruit juice concentrate, thawed

¾ cup superfine sugar
½ cup chilled whipping cream

FOR PEEL: Remove peel (yellow part only) from grapefruit using vegetable peeler. Cut peel into julienne strips. Combine with 2 cups water in heavy small saucepan. Bring to boil, reduce heat to low and simmer 5 minutes. Drain peel and rinse under cold water. Repeat blanching peel with remaining 2 cups water. Drain on paper towels.

Stir ¾ cup sugar and ¼ cup water in heavy small saucepan over low heat until sugar dissolves. Increase heat and boil without stirring until syrup registers

230°F on candy thermometer (thread stage). Remove syrup from heat. Add peel and cool 10 minutes. Stir in 2 tablespoons dark rum. Cool completely. *(Can be prepared 1 day ahead. Cover and refrigerate.)*

FOR SOUFFLÉS: Cut six 6x12-inch waxed-paper rectangles. Fold each rectangle in half lengthwise, forming a 3x12-inch strip. Wrap each strip around one ½-cup soufflé dish, forming 2-inch-high collar. Tie collar to dish using kitchen string. Spray insides of collars lightly with nonstick spray.

Combine ¼ cup cold water and rum in top of double boiler. Sprinkle gelatin over liquid. Let stand 10 minutes to soften. Whisk yolks into gelatin mixture. Whisk mixture over pan of boiling water until gelatin dissolves and mixture thickens slightly, about 2 minutes. Pour into large bowl and cool 5 minutes. Whisk in grapefruit juice concentrate.

Refrigerate mixture until just beginning to set, stirring occasionally, about 8 minutes. Remove mixture from refrigerator and set aside.

Using electric mixer fitted with clean dry beaters, beat egg whites in another large bowl until soft peaks form. Gradually beat in superfine sugar and continue beating until stiff and shiny. Whisk grapefruit mixture until smooth. Fold in ½ of egg whites to lighten mixture. Gently fold in remaining egg whites. In another large bowl, whip cream to soft peaks. Gently fold cream into grapefruit mixture. Carefully spoon mixture into prepared dishes. Smooth tops with spatula if necessary. Refrigerate until set, about 3 hours. *(Can be prepared 1 day ahead.)*

Drain candied peel on paper towels. Run small sharp knife between soufflés and collars to loosen. Remove string and collars. Garnish soufflés with candied grapefruit peel and serve.

FOOD TIPS FOR TYKES

ANY PARENT KNOWS IT CAN BE tough teaching kids good eating habits. Not only do mom and dad have to please finicky youngsters, but they also have to interpret the latest food news, much of which does not address the special needs of children. One resource that does is *A Healthy Head Start* (Henry Holt and Company, 1990) by Mary Abbott Hess, M.S., R.D.; Anne Elise Hunt; and Barbara Motenko Stone. It's available in bookstores across the country.

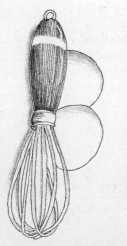

Peach Mousse in
Pine Nut Cookie Baskets

The cookie baskets are a delicious and beautiful way to serve this refreshing mousse. Press the warm cookies over a custard cup to form the bowl shape. The recipe makes about 16 baskets, so you'll have enough if a few break. For an even easier dessert, purchase some waffle cone "dishes" from a local ice cream parlor and fill them with the mousse.

8 SERVINGS

COOKIE BASKETS

⅔ cup sugar
½ cup (1 stick) unsalted butter
3 tablespoons water
2 tablespoons plus 2 teaspoons light corn syrup
Pinch of salt
1 cup blanched almonds, ground
½ cup pine nuts
6 tablespoons plus 2 teaspoons all-purpose flour
¼ teaspoon ground cinnamon

PEACH MOUSSE

2 teaspoons dark rum
1 teaspoon vanilla extract
⅛ teaspoon almond extract
1¼ teaspoons unflavored gelatin
1 pound ripe peaches, peeled, pitted
3 tablespoons sugar
3 egg yolks

¾ cup chilled whipping cream
½ cup powdered sugar
½ teaspoon grated lemon peel

Fresh mint sprigs (optional)

FOR COOKIE BASKETS: Preheat oven to 350°F. Cut out sixteen 8-inch foil squares. Butter foil. Bring sugar, butter, 3 tablespoons water, corn syrup and salt to boil in heavy medium saucepan over medium-high heat, stirring constantly. Add almonds, pine nuts, flour and cinnamon and return to boil, stirring constantly. Remove from heat.

Arrange 2 pieces of prepared foil on heavy large cookie sheet. Drop 1 rounded tablespoon batter on each piece of foil. Bake until cookies are light brown, about 9 minutes. Remove from oven. Immediately turn one cookie over onto inverted custard cup and, using oven mitts as aid, press foil with cookie loosely around cup to form basket. Quickly repeat with second cookie and second custard cup. Let stand until cookies harden, about 5 minutes. Remove cookies from cups; carefully peel off foil. In batches of 2, repeat with remaining batter and foil squares. *(Can be prepared 2 days ahead. Store in airtight containers at room temperature.)*

FOR MOUSSE: Combine rum, vanilla and almond extracts in small bowl. Sprinkle gelatin over and let soften at least 10 minutes. Puree peaches in processor. Pour into heavy medium saucepan. Add 3 tablespoons sugar and bring to simmer, stirring to dissolve sugar. Simmer 10 minutes. Whisk yolks in medium bowl to blend. Gradually whisk simmering puree into yolks. Return yolk mixture to same pan. Add gelatin mixture and stir over medium-low heat until candy thermometer registers 160°F, about 2 minutes. Transfer to large bowl and refrigerate until cold, stirring occasionally, about 40 minutes.

Whip cream with powdered sugar in large bowl until stiff peaks form. Whisk in lemon peel. Fold cream mixture into peach mixture in 2 additions. *(Can be prepared 1 day ahead. Cover mousse and refrigerate.)*

Arrange 1 cookie basket on each serving plate. Spoon mousse into baskets. Garnish with fresh mint and serve.

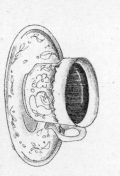

DESSERT REVERSE PHILOSOPHY

"I WISH I COULD PUT A CUTTING board across my Stair-Master so I could chop vegetables and climb stairs at the same time. Seriously, I believe cooking has radically shifted gears. We used to make butter sauces with herbs, now we make herb sauces with butter. The same reverse philosophy applies to dessert sauces. I no longer prepare *crème anglaise* decorated with a wee bit of raspberry puree. Instead, I puree fresh fruit in season and whisk in a tiny amount of crème anglaise to enrich it."

Norman Van Aken
Executive Chef: a Mano; Miami Beach
Author: A Feast of Sunlight

RASPBERRY AND COFFEE TIRAMISU

An unexpected combination of ingredients updates the classic Italian dessert. It is presented in individual servings here, but the ladyfingers, espresso and filling can be layered in a large dish and offered with the sauce on the side if you prefer.

6 SERVINGS

LADYFINGER ROUNDS
½ cup all-purpose flour
½ teaspoon finely ground coffee (preferably espresso)
3 extra-large eggs, separated, room temperature
5 tablespoons sugar
½ teaspoon vanilla extract

Powdered sugar

FILLING
3 tablespoons framboise eau-de-vie (clear raspberry brandy)
1 tablespoon instant espresso

powder or instant coffee granules

2 8-ounce packages cream cheese (preferably old-fashioned, low-salt cream cheese), room temperature

⅔ cup powdered sugar

1 6-ounce basket raspberries or 1½ cups frozen unsweetened, thawed, drained

¾ cup freshly brewed strong coffee (preferably espresso), room temperature

3 tablespoons sugar

Additional powdered sugar

Raspberry Sauce (see recipe)

Fresh mint

FOR LADYFINGER ROUNDS: Preheat oven to 350°F. Line 2 cookie sheets with parchment. Mix flour and ground coffee beans in small bowl. Using electric mixer, beat egg yolks and 4 tablespoons sugar in medium bowl until thick and slowly dissolving ribbon forms when beaters are lifted, about 4 minutes. Beat in vanilla. Mix in dry ingredients (batter will be thick). Using electric mixer fitted with clean dry beaters, beat egg whites until thick and foamy. Add remaining 1 tablespoon sugar and beat until whites are stiff but not dry. Fold into yolk mixture in 2 additions.

Drop batter by rounded tablespoons (8 per sheet) onto prepared sheets, spacing evenly. Sift powdered sugar thickly over rounds. Bake until rounds are golden brown on edges, about 16 minutes. Cool in pan on rack. Remove ladyfinger rounds from parchment. (Can be prepared 1 day ahead. Store in single layer in airtight container.)

FOR FILLING: Combine framboise and instant espresso in small bowl. Stir until espresso dissolves. Using electric mixer, beat cream cheese and ⅔ cup powdered sugar until light and fluffy. Beat in coffee mixture. Fold in 1 cup raspberries. Let stand at room temperature.

Combine coffee and 3 tablespoons sugar. Stir until sugar dissolves. Spoon 1 scant tablespoon coffee mixture over flat side of 1 ladyfinger round. Place coffee side up on plate. Spread ⅓ cup filling atop round. Spoon 1 scant tablespoon coffee mixture over flat side of second ladyfinger round. Place flat side down atop filling. Sprinkle with powdered sugar. Repeat with remaining ladyfinger rounds, coffee, filling and powdered sugar. Spoon raspberry sauce around desserts. Garnish with remaining raspberries and fresh mint and serve.

RASPBERRY SAUCE

MAKES ABOUT 1¼ CUPS

1 10-ounce package frozen raspberries in syrup, thawed

2 tablespoons framboise eau-de-vie

Puree raspberries and syrup in processor. Strain into small bowl to remove seeds. Stir in eau-de-vie. (Can be prepared 2 days ahead. Cover and refrigerate.)

STEAMED CRANBERRY-MARMALADE PUDDING WITH GRAND MARNIER HARD SAUCE

8 SERVINGS

1 cup unbleached all-purpose flour
1 teaspoon baking powder
½ teaspoon ground ginger
½ teaspoon ground nutmeg
¼ teaspoon salt
½ cup (1 stick) unsalted butter, room temperature
¾ cup sugar
2 large eggs
¼ cup sherry
½ cup orange marmalade
2 cups coarsely chopped cranberries

Grand Marnier Hard Sauce Rosettes (see recipe)
Candied Cranberries (see recipe)

Preheat oven to 350°F. Butter and flour 1-quart pudding mold or loaf pan. Sift first 5 ingredients into medium bowl. Using electric mixer, beat butter in large bowl until light and fluffy. Beat in sugar. Add eggs 1 at a time, beating well after each addition. Mix in dry ingredients alternately with sherry, beginning and ending with dry ingredients. Gently beat in marmalade. Carefully fold in chopped cranberries.

Spoon batter into prepared mold; smooth top with small spatula. Butter large sheet of foil. Cover pudding tightly with foil. Place pudding in Dutch oven or large baking pan. Pour enough hot water into pan to come halfway up sides of mold. Bake until small knife inserted near center of pudding comes out clean, about 2½ hours. Remove from water. Cool 10 minutes.

Run small sharp knife around edge of pudding to loosen. Turn out onto plate. (*Can be prepared 4 days ahead. Cool completely. Wrap tightly in plastic; chill. To reheat: Remove plastic; wrap* pudding *in foil. Place in 350°F oven until heated through, about 45 minutes.*)

Serve steamed pudding warm with Grand Marnier Hard Sauce Rosettes and Candied Cranberries.

CANDIED CRANBERRIES

MAKES ABOUT ⅓ CUP

¾ cup sugar
½ cup water
½ cup cranberries

Line small cookie sheet with waxed paper. Bring ½ cup sugar and water to boil in heavy medium saucepan, stirring until sugar dissolves. Continue boiling until mixture registers 238°F (soft-ball stage) on candy thermometer, about 6 minutes. Remove from heat; stir in cranberries. Let stand until cranberries are tender but still retain shape, about 3 minutes. Using slotted spoon, carefully transfer cranberries to prepared cookie sheet. Let stand until almost dry, about 20 minutes.

Place remaining ¼ cup sugar on plate. Roll cranberries in sugar until completely coated. Store cranberries in sugar *(Can be prepared 6 hours ahead.)*

DIABETES QUIZ

HEALTH AND NUTRITION ARE OF special concern to the 14 million Americans affected by diabetes. Unfortunately, nearly half don't realize they have the disorder. The American Diabetes Association has a quiz designed to alert you to symptoms if you think you might be at risk. For a free copy contact the ADA at 1660 Duke Street, Alexandria, VA 22314; 800-232-3472.

GRAND MARNIER HARD SAUCE ROSETTES

These make a pretty garnish for any steamed pudding. If you don't want to pipe the hard sauce, simply place it in a bowl and pass separately

MAKES 8 ROSETTES

½ cup (1 stick) unsalted butter, room temperature
1½ cups powdered sugar
2 tablespoons Grand Marnier or other orange liqueur

Line small cookie sheet with waxed paper. Using electric mixer, beat butter until light and fluffy. Add powdered sugar; beat until smooth. Gradually beat in liqueur. Transfer to pastry bag fitted with large star tip. Pipe 8 large rosettes onto prepared cookie sheet. Chill until set, about 1 hour. *(Can be prepared 3 days ahead. Wrap in plastic.)*

Cakes

Creating a delicious dessert is quite literally a piece of cake, thanks to the recipes that follow. From Strawberry Mousse Cake to Citrus Chiffon; from No-Fat Mocha Cake to Lemon Cheesecake with Fresh Berry Topping; from Angel Food Cake with Strawberry-Blueberry Sauce to No-Cholesterol Brownies, every one is as easy to make and delicate on the palate as it is beautiful and tempting.

STRAWBERRY MOUSSE CAKE

Flavored with just a hint of Grand Marnier and topped with whole fresh berries, this delicate dessert is a stunning conclusion to any occasion.

12 SERVINGS

SYRUP

6 tablespoons water
3 tablespoons sugar
2 tablespoons Grand Marnier or other orange liqueur

CAKE

8 large eggs
1 cup sugar
1 teaspoon vanilla extract
¼ teaspoon almond extract
1⅓ cups all-purpose flour
6 tablespoons (¾ stick) unsalted butter, melted, cooled

MOUSSE

2 12-ounce baskets strawberries, stemmed, chopped
1½ cups chilled whipping cream
6 tablespoons powdered sugar
1 tablespoon Grand Marnier or other orange liqueur
1 teaspoon vanilla extract

TOPPING

2 cups chilled whipping cream
3 tablespoons powdered sugar
1 tablespoon Grand Marnier or other orange liqueur
1 teaspoon vanilla extract

16 large strawberries, stemmed

FOR SYRUP: Stir 6 tablespoons water and sugar in heavy small saucepan over medium heat until sugar dissolves. Mix in Grand Marnier. (*Can be prepared 1 week ahead. Cover and refrigerate.*)

FOR CAKE: Preheat oven to 350°F. Butter two 9-inch round pans with 2-inch-high sides. Line bottoms of pans with waxed-paper rounds. Butter and flour waxed-paper rounds.

Whisk eggs and sugar in large bowl set over saucepan of simmering water until mixture is just warm to touch.

Remove from over water. Add vanilla and almond extracts. Using electric mixer, beat mixture at medium-high speed until tripled in volume, about 7 minutes. Sift half of flour over egg mixture and fold in. Repeat with remaining flour. Fold 1 cup batter into butter. Fold butter mixture back into remaining cake batter. Divide batter evenly between prepared cake pans. Bake until tester inserted into centers comes out clean, about 25 minutes. Cool cakes in pans 5 minutes. Turn cakes out onto racks and cool completely. Peel off paper. (*Can be prepared 1 day ahead. Wrap tightly and store at room temperature.*)

FOR MOUSSE: Puree half of berries in processor or blender. Using electric mixer, beat cream, sugar, Grand Marnier and vanilla extract in large bowl until stiff peaks form. Fold in pureed berries and remaining chopped berries.

FOR TOPPING: Using electric mixer,

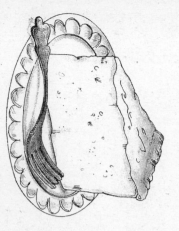

beat whipping cream, sugar, Grand Marnier and vanilla extract in large bowl until stiff peaks form.

Cut each cake layer in half horizontally. Place 1 layer on platter. Brush with ¼ of syrup. Spread ⅓ of mousse on cake. Repeat layering with cake, syrup and mousse 2 more times. Top with last cake layer. Brush with remaining syrup. Spread topping over top and sides of cake. Arrange whole berries around top edge of cake; chill. (*Can be made 6 hours ahead. Cover with cake dome and chill.*)

MARZIPAN-TOPPED STRAWBERRY LAYER CAKE

This cake, also called fraisier (French for "strawberry plant"), is usually made with almonds, but here pistachios are used. The delicate cake is layered with fresh strawberries and a mousse-like white chocolate buttercream, then topped with marzipan.

10 SERVINGS

CAKE

2 large eggs, room temperature
⅓ cup plus 2 tablespoons sugar
½ cup ground unsalted pistachios
½ cup unbleached all-purpose flour
¼ teaspoon baking powder
4 large egg whites, room temperature

BUTTERCREAM

6 large egg yolks
⅓ cup sugar
2 tablespoons unbleached all-purpose flour
1½ cups half-and-half
8 ounces imported white chocolate (such as Lindt), chopped
2 teaspoons vanilla extract
1 cup (2 sticks) unsalted butter, room temperature
5 tablespoons fraise or framboise eau-de-vie (clear strawberry or raspberry brandies) or other brandy

6 tablespoons strawberry jam
3 1-pint baskets strawberries, stemmed
7 ounces marzipan
Green food coloring
Powdered sugar
2 ounces imported white chocolate (such as Lindt), chopped
4 strawberries, cut in half through stem end

FOR CAKE: Position rack in center of oven and preheat to 350°F. Butter 9-inch square pan with 2-inch-high sides. Line bottom with parchment paper. Butter and flour parchment.

Using electric mixer, beat eggs and ⅓ cup sugar on high speed in large bowl until slowly dissolving ribbon forms when beaters are lifted, about 4 minutes. Mix nuts, flour and baking powder in medium bowl. Fold nut mixture into egg mixture. Using clean beaters, beat egg whites in medium bowl until soft peaks form. Gradually add remaining 2 tablespoons sugar and beat until stiff peaks form. Fold whites into batter in 2 additions. Transfer batter to prepared pan. Bake until tester inserted in center comes out clean, about 18 minutes. Cool cake in pan on rack 5 minutes. Cut cake out around cake in pan. Turn cake out onto rack. Peel off parchment; cool cake completely.

FOR BUTTERCREAM: Whisk yolks, sugar and flour in medium bowl until well blended. Bring half-and-half to simmer in heavy medium saucepan.

Slowly pour hot half-and-half into egg mixture, whisking constantly. Return egg mixture to same saucepan and cook until mixture is very thick and boils, whisking constantly. Transfer mixture to medium bowl. Add 8 ounces white chocolate and vanilla extract and stir until chocolate melts and mixture is smooth. Press plastic wrap on surface of pastry cream to prevent skin from forming; cool. (*Can be prepared 1 day ahead. Refrigerate. Bring to room temperature before continuing.*)

Using electric mixer, beat 1 cup unsalted butter and 1 tablespoon brandy in large bowl until fluffy. Add pastry cream ¼ cup at a time, beating after each addition until just blended.

Melt jam in heavy small saucepan over medium heat. Stir remaining 4 tablespoons brandy into jam. Cut cake horizontally into 2 even layers. Place 1 layer on 8-inch cardboard square. Brush half of jam over. Spread 1 cup

buttercream over jam. Cover buttercream layer completely with whole strawberries, stem end down. Set aside ½ cup buttercream; spoon remaining buttercream over berries, spreading buttercream between and around berries. Spread remaining jam over second cake layer. Place cake, jam side down, atop buttercream. Press cake gently to adhere. Refrigerate cake until buttercream is firm. (*Can be prepared 1 day ahead. Cover cake and remaining buttercream separately and chill. Bring buttercream to room temperature before continuing.*)

Knead marzipan and 2 drops green coloring in large bowl until color is evenly distributed. Dust work surface with powdered sugar Roll out marzipan on sugar to 12-inch-diameter circle, sprinkling with powdered sugar as needed to prevent sticking. Spread reserved ½ cup buttercream over top of cake. Using rolling pin as aid, drape marzipan over top of cake. Press gently to adhere

Trim marzipan flush with top of cake; reserve trimmings. Brush excess powdered sugar off marzipan. Using long sharp knife, cut ⅓ inch off each side of dessert to expose strawberries. Cut marzipan trimmings into leaf shapes using small cutter.

Melt 2 ounces white chocolate in heavy small saucepan over low heat. Transfer chocolate to small parchment cone. Cut off tip to form small opening. Pipe the word *Fraisier* atop marzipan layer. Garnish with strawberry halves and marzipan leaves. Refrigerate. (*Can be prepared 4 hours ahead.*)

SHERRY-SOAKED ALMOND CAKE WITH MIXED BERRIES

Two of Spain's best-known ingredients come together in this luscious dessert.

8 SERVINGS

CAKE
1 cup toasted whole almonds (about 5¼ ounces)
1 cup cake flour
1½ teaspoons baking powder
10 tablespoons (1¼ sticks) unsalted butter, room temperature
⅔ cup plus 1 tablespoon sugar
7 ounces almond paste, cut into small pieces
1½ teaspoons vanilla extract
3 large eggs
3 large eggs, separated

SYRUP
1¼ cups cream sherry
⅓ cup sugar
¼ cup (½ stick) butter
¼ teaspoon almond extract

Lightly sweetened whipped cream
1 ½-pint basket boysenberries, blackberries or raspberries
1 1-pint basket strawberries, hulled, halved

FOR CAKE: Preheat oven to 325°F. Butter and flour 10-inch-diameter tube pan with 3½-inch-high sides. Finely grind toasted almonds in processor. Blend in flour and baking powder. Using electric mixer, beat butter and ⅔ cup sugar in large bowl until blended. Beat in almond paste a few pieces at a time. Add vanilla extract and beat until mixture resembles paste. Add 3 whole eggs 1 at a time, beating well after each addition. Beat in 3 egg yolks. Stir in dry ingredients. Using electric mixer fitted with clean dry beaters, beat 3 egg whites in medium bowl to soft peaks. Gradually add remaining 1 tablespoon sugar and beat until stiff but not dry. Fold whites into batter in 2 additions.

Pour batter into prepared pan (batter will fill pan less than halfway). Bake until tester inserted near center of cake comes out clean, about 45 minutes. Cool cake in pan on rack 1 hour. Pierce top of cake all over with wooden skewer.

FOR SYRUP: Combine cream sherry, sugar and butter in heavy small saucepan. Stir over low heat until sugar dissolves. Simmer until reduced to 1 cup, about 15 minutes. Mix in almond extract. Let syrup stand until just cool. Brush half of syrup over cake in pan. Let cake stand 1 hour. Turn cake out onto platter. Reheat remaining syrup just until butter melts. Pierce more holes in cake. Brush syrup over cake. Let cake stand 30 minutes. *(Can be prepared 1 day ahead. Cover cake and let stand at room temperature.)*

Cut cake into wedges. Garnish with dollops of sweetened whipped cream and berries and serve.

ANGEL FOOD CAKE WITH STRAWBERRY-BLUEBERRY SAUCE (COVER RECIPE)

10 TO 12 SERVINGS

SAUCE

2 12-ounce baskets strawberries, hulled
1 12-ounce basket blueberries or
1 12-ounce package frozen unsweetened blueberries

⅓ cup sugar
1 tablespoon fresh lemon juice
¼ cup amaretto liqueur

CAKE

1¼ cups sifted cake flour
2 teaspoons vanilla extract
2 teaspoons fresh lemon juice
½ teaspoon almond extract
14 large egg whites, room temperature
1½ teaspoons cream of tartar
½ teaspoon salt
1⅔ cups sugar

Whole strawberries (optional)

FOR SAUCE: Place half of strawberries in medium bowl. Crush with fork or potato masher. Slice remaining strawberries and add to bowl. Add half of blueberries to same bowl. Place remaining blueberries in medium saucepan and crush; add sugar and 1 tablespoon lemon juice. Stir over medium heat until sugar dissolves and juices become syrupy, about 4 minutes. Cool. Add to strawberry mixture.

Stir in amaretto. Let stand 20 minutes. *(Can be prepared 8 hours ahead. Cover and refrigerate.)*

FOR CAKE: Position rack in center of oven and preheat to 300°F. Sift flour once more into medium bowl. Combine vanilla, lemon juice and almond extract in small bowl. Using electric mixer, beat whites in large bowl at medium speed until frothy. Add cream of tartar and salt and beat until soft peaks form. Add sugar ⅓ cup at a time and continue to beat until whites are stiff but not dry. Fold in vanilla mixture. Sift flour over in 4 batches, gently folding in each addition.

Spoon batter into ungreased 10-inch angel food cake pan. Bake until top of cake is golden brown and springy to touch, about 1 hour 10 minutes. Invert cake pan over neck of narrow bottle and cool cake completely. Run knife around edge of pan to loosen cake. Turn out onto waxed-paper-lined plate. *(Can be prepared 8 hours ahead. Cover and let stand at room temperature.)*

Using serrated knife, cut cake into wedges. Place on plates. Spoon berry sauce over. Garnish each with whole strawberry if desired and serve

CITRUS CHIFFON CAKE

Sponge cakes are a characteristic Passover tradition—but they don't have to be dry. This one isn't, thanks to fresh orange and lemon juice. Serve plain or with fruit.

8 SERVINGS

CITRUS CURD

5 egg yolks
½ cup plus 2 tablespoons sugar
6 tablespoons fresh orange juice
2 tablespoons fresh lemon juice
1½ tablespoons grated orange peel
¼ cup (½ stick) unsalted margarine, cut into 4 pieces, room temperature

CAKE

½ cup almonds (about 3 ounces)
1¼ cups potato starch
7 large egg yolks
1¼ cups sugar
2 tablespoons freshly grated orange peel
¼ cup fresh orange juice

¼ cup fresh lemon juice
½ cup (1 stick) unsalted margarine, melted, room temperature
9 large egg whites
¼ teaspoon salt

1 1-pint basket strawberries, thinly sliced
Nondairy topping
5 strawberries with stems

FOR CURD: Whisk yolks, sugar, juices and orange peel together in top of double boiler. Cook over boiling water until curd thickens to consistency of yogurt, stirring frequently; about 15 minutes. Add margarine 1 piece at a time and whisk until melted and curd is smooth. Pour mixture into medium bowl. Press plastic wrap onto surface of curd to prevent skin from forming. Refrigerate overnight. (*Curd can be prepared up to 3 days ahead.*)

FOR CAKE: Preheat oven to 350°F. Coarsely grind nuts in processor. Combine with potato starch in small bowl.

Using electric mixer, beat yolks and 1 cup sugar in large bowl until pale yellow and slowly dissolving ribbon forms when beaters are lifted. Add orange peel. Fold in nut mixture alternately with juices, beginning and ending with nut mixture. Fold in margarine.

Using clean dry beaters, beat egg whites and salt in large bowl until soft peaks form. Gradually add remaining ¼ cup sugar and continue beating until stiff but not dry. Fold ¼ of whites into yolk mixture to lighten. Gently fold remaining whites into yolk mixture.

Pour batter into ungreased 10-inch-diameter tube pan. Bake until cake is golden brown and toothpick inserted near center comes out clean, about 40 minutes. Cool in pan inverted onto rack. (Can be prepared 6 hours ahead.)

Remove pan. Cut cake horizontally into 3 layers using serrated knife. Place bottom cake layer on platter and spread with ½ of citrus curd. Arrange ½ of sliced strawberries over curd. Top with second cake layer, then remaining curd, remaining strawberry slices and final cake layer. (Can be prepared 2 hours ahead.) Pipe 5 rosettes of non-dairy topping around top of cake. Place whole strawberry atop each rosette.

ORANGE-ALMOND CAKE WITH PEACHES AND AMARETTO WHIPPED CREAM

Honey enhances the flavor of the cake and glaze. Serve the cake either warm or at room temperature.

8 SERVINGS

GLAZE

⅓ cup honey
⅓ cup amaretto liqueur
⅓ cup orange juice

CAKE

1 cup almonds
2 cups all-purpose flour
2 teaspoons baking powder
¼ teaspoon salt
½ cup honey
½ cup orange juice
½ cup milk
¼ cup amaretto liqueur
¾ cup (1½ sticks) unsalted butter, room temperature
1 cup sugar
1 tablespoon grated orange peel
2 eggs, room temperature

4 large peaches, peeled, pitted, sliced
3 tablespoons sugar
2 teaspoons lemon juice
Amaretto Whipped Cream (see recipe)
Toasted sliced almonds

FOR GLAZE: Bring honey, liqueur and orange juice to boil in heavy small saucepan. Reduce heat and simmer glaze until reduced to ⅓ cup. Cool. (*Can be prepared 1 day ahead. Cover and refrigerate. Bring glaze to room temperature before using.*)

FOR CAKE: Preheat oven to 350°F. Butter and flour 12-cup bundt pan. Finely grind 1 cup almonds in processor. Sift flour, baking powder and salt into bowl. Mix in almonds. Combine honey, orange juice, milk and liqueur in small bowl. Using electric mixer, cream butter with 1 cup sugar and orange peel in large bowl until light and fluffy. Add eggs 1 at a time, beating well after each addition. Mix in dry ingredients alternately with orange juice mixture, beating just until combined. Spoon batter into prepared pan. Bake until tester inserted near center comes out clean, about 1 hour Transfer cake in pan to rack and cool 15 minutes.

Invert cake onto plate. Spoon glaze over warm cake, allowing glaze to run down sides. Cool cake until just warm. Toss peaches with 3 tablespoons sugar and lemon juice. Arrange peaches around edge of cake. Fill center with some of whipped cream. Sprinkle cake with sliced almonds. Slice cake and serve with peaches and whipped cream.

AMARETTO WHIPPED CREAM

MAKES ABOUT 2 CUPS

1 cup chilled whipping cream
2 tablespoons sugar
2 tablespoons amaretto liqueur

Using electric mixer, whip all ingredients together in medium bowl to stiff peaks. (Can be prepared 4 hours ahead; cover and refrigerate.)

NO-CHOLESTEROL BROWNIES

MAKES 16

1½ cups sugar
1 cup all-purpose flour
¾ cup unsweetened cocoa powder
1 teaspoon baking powder
¼ teaspoon salt
¾ cup vegetable oil
4 egg whites, beaten to blend
2 teaspoons vanilla
⅔ cup chopped walnuts

Preheat oven to 350°F. Grease 8-inch square pan with 2-inch-high sides. Combine first 5 ingredients in large bowl. Add oil, egg whites and vanilla and blend. Stir in walnuts. Transfer to prepared pan. Bake until brownies are slightly puffed in center and edges are beginning to brown, about 30 minutes. Cover hot brownies in pan with foil and chill overnight. Cut brownies into 16 2-inch squares. (Can be prepared 3 days ahead. Store in airtight container)

LEMON CHEESECAKE WITH FRESH BERRY TOPPING

These smooth and creamy cheesecakes have no graham cracker crust, making them a snap to prepare.

MAKES TWO 9-INCH CHEESECAKES

10 8-ounce packages cream cheese, room temperature
2 cups sugar
2 tablespoons Grand Marnier, other orange liqueur or orange juice

8 large eggs
2 cups sour cream
¾ cup plus 2 tablespoons fresh lemon juice
4 tablespoons grated lemon peel

2 ½-pint baskets raspberries
2 ½-pint baskets blackberries
½ cup apricot preserves
3 tablespoons water

Preheat oven to 300°F. Generously butter two 9-inch-diameter springform pans with 2¾-inch-high sides. Using electric mixer, beat cream cheese in large bowl until light. Add sugar and Grand Marnier and beat until thoroughly combined. Add eggs 1 at a time, beating well after each addition. Fold in sour cream, lemon juice and lemon peel. Divide batter between prepared pans. Bake cheesecakes until outsides are set but centers still move slightly when pans are shaken, about 1 hour 15 minutes. Transfer cheesecakes to racks to cool. Cover with plastic wrap and refrigerate cheesecakes overnight.

Run small sharp knife around pan sides to loosen cheesecakes if necessary. Release pan sides. Transfer cheesecakes to platters. Toss berries gently in large bowl. Mound berries on cheesecakes, leaving 1-inch border. Heat preserves with 3 tablespoons water in heavy small saucepan over medium heat, stirring until melted. Brush warm glaze over berries. (Can be prepared 1 day ahead. Cover loosely and refrigerate.) Cut into wedges and serve

NO-FAT MOCHA CAKE

The secret to this rich and fudgy cake is good-quality unsweetened cocoa powder, which provides the smooth taste of chocolate without the fat.

6 TO 8 SERVINGS

1 cup all-purpose flour
⅓ cup plus 2 tablespoons unsweetened cocoa powder
1 teaspoon instant espresso powder or instant coffee powder

1 teaspoon baking powder
1 teaspoon baking soda
6 large egg whites, room temperature
1⅓ cups firmly packed golden brown sugar
1 cup coffee-flavored nonfat yogurt
1 teaspoon vanilla extract

1 teaspoon powdered sugar
½ teaspoon ground cinnamon

Preheat oven to 350°F. Line bottom of 9-inch-diameter cake pan with 1¾-inch-high sides with waxed paper. Spray pan and paper with vegetable oil spray (or oil pan and paper lightly). Dust pan with flour; tap out excess.

Sift 1 cup flour, ⅓ cup plus 1 tablespoon cocoa, espresso powder, baking powder and baking soda into medium bowl. Using electric mixer, beat egg whites, brown sugar, yogurt and vanilla in large bowl until blended, about 1 minute. Mix in dry ingredients. Transfer batter to prepared pan. Bake cake until tester inserted into center comes out clean, about 35 minutes. Cool in pan on rack 15 minutes. Cut around pan sides to loosen cake. Turn out onto plate. Peel off paper and cool completely.

Combine remaining 1 tablespoon cocoa powder, powdered sugar and cinnamon in small bowl. Sprinkle over cake before serving.

CARROT AND ALMOND CHIFFON CAKE

8 SERVINGS

2½ cups blanched almonds, lightly toasted
1 cup matzo meal
½ cup potato starch
1½ teaspoons cinnamon
¼ teaspoon ground ginger

10 large eggs, separated
1½ cups sugar
¼ cup vegetable oil
¼ cup fresh orange juice
1½ cups finely grated carrots (about 2 large)
2 tablespoons grated orange peel

1 teaspoon fresh lemon juice
¼ teaspoon salt

Blackberries or boysenberries

Preheat oven to 350°F. Lightly oil 10-inch-diameter tube pan. Grind almonds in food processor. Coat bottom and sides of pan with ½ cup ground almonds. Mix 1½ cups ground almonds with matzo meal, potato starch and spices in medium bowl.

Using electric mixer, beat egg yolks and 1 cup sugar in large bowl until pale yellow and doubled in volume, about 3 minutes. Beat in oil. Mix in dry ingredients alternately with orange juice. Mix in carrots and orange peel.

Using electric mixer fitted with clean dry beaters, beat egg whites, lemon juice and salt in another large bowl until soft peaks form. Gradually beat in remaining ½ cup sugar and continue beating until stiff but not dry. Fold ⅓ of egg whites into batter to lighten mixture. Gently fold in remaining egg whites.

Pour batter into prepared pan. Sprinkle remaining almonds over top of cake. Bake until toothpick inserted into center of cake comes out clean, about 45 minutes. Cool in pan on rack. Turn cake out onto plate. (*Can be prepared 4 hours ahead. Store at room temperature.*) Garnish with berries.

Pies, Tarts & Pastries

With their vividly colored fillings, crisp crusts and eye-catching assemblies, pies, tarts and pastries tempt like nothing else. Yet, as the recipes that follow prove, such classic baked goods can indeed be both light and easy. From Tropical Lime Mousse Pie to Triple Berry Tart; from Phyllo Purses with Raspberry Sauce to Peach Tart with Almond Crust, these desserts end a meal with the right light touch.

FRESH RASPBERRY PIE

In this summer treat, cinnamon-flavored pastry encloses a delicious filling.

8 SERVINGS

PASTRY

2½ cups all-purpose flour
¼ cup firmly packed light brown sugar
1 teaspoon ground cinnamon
½ teaspoon salt
½ cup (1 stick) chilled unsalted butter, cut into pieces
½ cup chilled solid vegetable shortening, cut into pieces
6 tablespoons (about) ice water

FILLING

1⅓ cups plus 1 tablespoon sugar
7 tablespoons cornstarch
1 tablespoon grated lemon peel
6 cups fresh raspberries
⅛ teaspoon ground cinnamon

FOR PASTRY: Blend first 4 ingredients in processor. Add butter and shortening and cut in using on/off turns until mixture resembles coarse meal. Blend in enough ice water to form moist clumps. Gather dough into ball. Divide in half. Flatten each piece into disk. Wrap in plastic; chill at least 1 hour or overnight.

FOR FILLING: Preheat oven to 375°F. Mix 1⅓ cups sugar, cornstarch and lemon peel in large bowl. Add berries and toss to combine.

Roll out 1 dough piece on lightly floured surface to 12-inch round. Transfer dough to 9-inch round glass pie dish with 1¼-inch-high sides; trim edges. Roll out remaining dough to thickness of ⅛ inch. Using 3-inch heart-shaped cookie cutter, cut dough into hearts. Gather scraps, reroll and cut out more hearts. Spoon filling into pie. Brush edge of pastry with water. Slightly overlap hearts around edge of pie, tips pointing toward center. Repeat with remaining

hearts, arranging in rings and covering top of pie but leaving space between rings for steam to escape. Using wooden skewer, carefully pierce hole in center of each heart.

Place pie on cookie sheet. Bake until top is golden brown and juices bubble, about 1 hour. Transfer pie to rack. Mix remaining 1 tablespoon sugar and cinnamon in small bowl. Sprinkle over pie. Cool before serving.

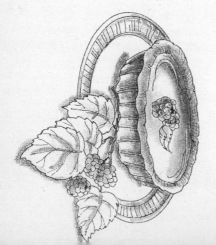

Triple Berry Tart

This is a variation of a tart at an Alsatian brasserie on the Ile St.-Louise in Paris. Blackberries, strawberries and blueberries, or any trio of fresh seasonal berries will do.

6 SERVINGS

CRUST

1¾ cups all-purpose flour
⅓ cup sugar
1 tablespoon grated lemon peel
½ teaspoon salt
¾ cup (1½ sticks) chilled unsalted butter, cut into pieces
2 large egg yolks
1 tablespoon fresh lemon juice
1 teaspoon vanilla extract
1 tablespoon (about) water

FILLING

⅓ cup red currant jelly
¼ cup raspberry jam
2 tablespoons framboise eau-de-vie (clear raspberry brandy), kirsch (clear cherry brandy) or orange juice
1 ½-pint basket blackberries or boysenberries
1 1-pint basket strawberries, hulled
½ cup (about) fresh blueberries

FOR CRUST: Mix flour, sugar, lemon peel and salt in large bowl. Add butter pieces and blend in using fingertips until mixture resembles coarse meal. Whisk egg yolks, lemon juice and vanilla extract in small bowl to blend. Add to flour mixture and stir until moist clumps form, adding water by tablespoons if mixture is dry. Gather dough into ball and flatten into disk. Wrap dough tightly in plastic and refrigerate 3 hours.

Roll dough out on lightly floured surface to 13-inch round. Transfer dough to 9-inch-diameter tart pan with removable bottom. Press dough onto bottom and up sides; trim edges. Pierce bottom of dough all over with fork. Refrigerate 2 hours.

Preheat oven to 425°F. Line crust with aluminum foil. Fill crust with dried beans or pie weights. Bake crust 10 minutes. Remove aluminum foil and dried beans. Bake crust until golden brown, about 20 minutes more. Transfer crust to rack and cool.

FOR FILLING: Cook red currant jelly, raspberry jam and brandy in heavy small saucepan over medium-high heat until thick, stirring frequently, about 3 minutes. Brush some of jam glaze over bottom of tart. Arrange circle of blackberries in ring around inside of tart edge. Arrange strawberries in ring, pointed ends up, inside ring of blackberries. Fill center of tart with blueberries. Brush more jam glaze over all berries. (*Tart can be prepared 2 hours ahead. Let stand at room temperature.*) Cut into wedges and serve.

NECTARINE AND MASCARPONE TARTLETS

In this sophisticated dessert, mascarpone (the nutty, creamy cheese from Italy) is flavored with kirsch, put into a crisp, light crust and topped with nectarine slices.

4 SERVINGS

CRUST

1 cup all-purpose flour
2 teaspoons sugar
½ teaspoon grated lemon peel
⅛ teaspoon salt
7 tablespoons chilled unsalted butter, cut into pieces
1 egg yolk
2 tablespoons cold water

GLAZE

¾ cup peach preserves
2 teaspoons kirsch (clear cherry brandy) or other brandy
1 teaspoon fresh lemon juice

FILLING

6 ounces mascarpone cheese*
¼ cup powdered sugar
2 teaspoons kirsch or other brandy
1 teaspoon vanilla extract
4 small nectarines, pitted, sliced
4 fresh mint sprigs (optional)

FOR CRUST: Combine flour, sugar, lemon peel and salt in processor. Add butter and process using on/off turns until mixture resembles coarse meal. Add yolk and 2 tablespoons water and process until large moist clumps form. Gather dough into ball; flatten into disk. Wrap in plastic and chill 30 minutes. *(Can be prepared 2 days ahead. Let dough soften slightly at room temperature before continuing.)*

Divide dough into quarters. Form each quarter into ball, then roll out each quarter to 6-inch round. Transfer rounds to four 4-inch-diameter tartlet pans with 1⅛-inch-high sides and removable bottoms. Gently press rounds into place. Trim edges. Pierce bottom of crusts with fork. Freeze until dough is very firm, about 30 minutes.

Preheat oven to 400°F. Bake crusts until golden, about 15 minutes. Cool crusts completely. *(Crusts can be prepared up to 1 day ahead. Cover and store at room temperature.)*

FOR GLAZE: Bring peach preserves, kirsch and lemon juice to boil in heavy small saucepan. Strain. Cool slightly.

FOR FILLING: Whisk mascarpone cheese, powdered sugar, kirsch and vanilla extract in small bowl until smooth. Brush insides of crusts with glaze Divide filling among crusts. Spread filling evenly. Arrange nectarine slices attractively atop filling. Brush nectarines with glaze.

Refrigerate tartlets until filling is set, about 30 minutes. *(Can be prepared up to 4 hours ahead.)* Remove tartlets from pans and garnish with fresh mint sprigs if desired.

*Italian cream cheese available at Italian markets and some specialty foods stores. If unavailable, blend 8 ounces cream cheese with ¼ cup whipping cream and 2½ tablespoons sour cream. Use ¾ cup of mixture for recipe.

PEACH-FRANGIPANE TART

Sophisticated and simple—even more so with the help of a purchased pie crust.

6 SERVINGS

1 All Ready Pie Crust (half of 15-ounce package), room temperature
2 tablespoons all-purpose flour
¾ cup slivered blanched almonds (about 3½ ounces)
⅓ cup sugar
3 tablespoons amaretto or other almond-flavored liqueur
2 tablespoons (¼ stick) unsalted butter, room temperature
1 egg

5 peaches
½ cup peach or apricot preserves

Preheat oven to 450°F. Open crust on work surface Sprinkle with 1 tablespoon flour. Rub flour over crust, rubbing out creases. Arrange floured side down in 9-inch-diameter tart pan with removable sides. Trim and finish edges. Pierce all over with fork. Bake until light brown, about 10 minutes. Cool on rack. Reduce oven temperature to 400°F.

Finely grind slivered almonds in processor. Add remaining 1 tablespoon flour, sugar, 2 tablespoons amaretto and butter and puree. Add egg and process until well blended. Pour into crust. Bake until filling begins to brown and is springy to touch, about 15 minutes. Cool on rack. (*Can be prepared 6 hours ahead. Let stand at room temperature.*)

Bring medium pot of water to boil. Add peaches and blanch 30 seconds. Transfer to bowl of cold water, using slotted spoon. Peel peaches. Cut into slices. Drain well. Combine preserves and 1 tablespoon amaretto in heavy small saucepan. Bring to boil, stirring to melt preserves. Boil until slightly thickened, about 30 seconds. Brush some preserves over tart filling. Arrange peaches atop preserves in concentric circles, overlapping slices. Brush with remaining preserves. (*Can be prepared 3 hours ahead. Store at room temperature.*)

TROPICAL LIME MOUSSE PIE

This Caribbean-inspired dessert is perfect after a spicy barbecue.

8 SERVINGS

CRUST

8 whole graham crackers
½ cup sweetened flaked coconut
7 tablespoons butter, melted

FILLING

¼ cup amber (gold) rum
1½ teaspoons unflavored gelatin

4 large eggs
1 cup sugar
⅔ cup fresh lime juice
3 tablespoons grated lime peel
1 cup chilled whipping cream
Sweetened flaked coconut, toasted

FOR CRUST: Preheat oven to 350°F Process graham crackers in processor until finely ground. Add coconut and butter and pulse to blend. Press crumb mixture on bottom and 1¾ inches up sides of 8-inch-diameter springform pan. Bake until golden brown on edges, about 10 minutes. Cool completely.

FOR FILLING: Place rum in small bowl. Sprinkle gelatin over. Let stand 10 minutes to soften. Whisk eggs, sugar and lime juice in heavy small saucepan over medium-high heat until mixture thickens and just comes to boil, about 4 minutes. Remove from heat. Add gelatin mixture and stir until gelatin melts. Mix in 2 tablespoons lime peel. Refrigerate mixture until cold but not set, stirring occasionally, about 30 minutes.

Whip chilled cream until soft peaks form. Fold whipped cream into lime mixture. Pour filling into crust. Refrigerate until filling is set, about 3 hours. Sprinkle pie with toasted coconut and remaining 1 tablespoon lime peel. Cut into wedges and serve.
(Can be prepared 1 day ahead.)

LEMON TOFU AND GINGER SILK PIE

For the smoothest filling, be sure to use a soft style of tofu, such as Japanese.

8 SERVINGS

CRUST
¾ cup finely ground gingersnap cookies (about 14)
4 teaspoons melted unsalted butter
1 teaspoon water

FILLING
¾ cup water
½ cup sugar
1 tablespoon grated peeled fresh ginger
1 envelope unflavored gelatin
⅔ cup fresh lemon juice
1 teaspoon grated lemon peel
1 pound soft tofu, drained, cut into pieces
1 cup plain lowfat yogurt
2 tablespoons finely chopped crystallized ginger

FOR CRUST: Preheat oven to 350°F. Combine gingersnap crumbs, butter and water in small bowl. Use fingers to press crumb mixture onto bottom and up sides of 9-inch pie plate. Bake crust 5 minutes. Cool on rack.

FOR FILLING: Stir water, sugar and fresh ginger in heavy small saucepan over low heat, stirring until sugar dissolves. Cover and let stand 10 minutes. Sprinkle gelatin over lemon juice in small cup. Let stand until gelatin softens, about 10 minutes.

Strain syrup through sieve into medium saucepan, pressing on solids with back of spoon. Add gelatin mixture to syrup and stir over low heat until gelatin dissolves, about 1 minute; do not boil. Pour into medium bowl. Add lemon peel. Set bowl over larger bowl filled with ice and water. Cool gelatin mixture until just beginning to thicken, stirring frequently, about 12 minutes. Remove bowl from over water.

Meanwhile, blend drained tofu pieces and yogurt in processor until very smooth, about 4 minutes.

Add gelatin mixture to tofu and blend until combined. Return mixture to bowl and set again over ice water bath. Let cool until mixture begins to mound on spoon, stirring frequently, about 25 minutes.

Spoon pie filling into prepared crust. Refrigerate until filling is set, at least 4 hours or overnight. Sprinkle crystallized ginger over pie. Cut pie into wedges and serve.

Lime Tart with Berry Sauce

The lime curd that fills this tart has much less butter and fewer eggs than most.

6 SERVINGS

FILLING

1½ cups sugar
¼ cup plus 1 teaspoon cornstarch
Pinch of salt
1¼ cups water
10 tablespoons fresh lime juice
1 tablespoon plus 1 teaspoon grated lime peel
4 egg yolks, beaten to blend
2 tablespoons (¼ stick) unsalted butter

SAUCE

1 16-ounce package frozen sliced strawberries with sugar, thawed
1½ tablespoons sugar
2 ½-pint baskets fresh blackberries

½ 15-ounce package All Ready Pie Crust (1 crust), room temperature
teaspoon all-purpose flour
Very thin lime slices

FOR FILLING: Combine sugar, cornstarch and salt in heavy medium saucepan. Stir in water, lime juice and peel. Mix in yolks. Bring to boil over medium heat, stirring constantly. Boil 1 minute, stirring constantly. Remove from heat, add butter and stir until melted. Press plastic onto surface of filling and chill well.

FOR SAUCE: Combine strawberries and sugar in heavy medium saucepan. Boil until mixture is very syrupy and coats spoon thinly, stirring occasionally, about 6 minutes. Remove from heat and stir in 1 basket blackberries; cool. (*Filling and sauce can be made 1 day ahead. Cover sauce and store both in refrigerator.*)

Preheat oven to 425°F. Let refrigerated crust stand at room temperature 20 minutes. Unfold crust and press out fold lines. Sprinkle with flour; spread flour over. Arrange floured side down in 9-inch-diameter tart pan with removable bottom. Fold in edges. Pierce all over with fork. Bake crust until brown, pressing up sides with back of fork if they slide down, about 12 minutes. Cool completely on rack.

Spoon filling into crust. Cover and chill until set, at least 3 hours. (*Can be prepared 6 hours ahead. Keep chilled.*)

Make 1 cut in each lime slice from center to edge; twist each slice. Alternate blackberries and lime twists around edge of tart. Cut tart into wedges, spoon sauce over and serve.

EASY APRICOT ALMOND TART

To peel apricots, blanch about 20 seconds. Drain and rinse with cold water, then slip off the peels with a paring knife.

6 SERVINGS

1 9-inch refrigerated ready pie crust, room temperature
1 teaspoon (generous) all-purpose flour
¼ cup apricot preserves
¾ cup slivered almonds, very finely chopped in processor
7 to 9 apricots, peeled, halved
⅓ cup sugar
1 tablespoon butter

Preheat oven to 450°F. Unfold crust and press out fold lines. Sprinkle with flour and gently spread flour over crust. Arrange floured side down in 9-inch-diameter tart pan with removable bottom. Trim edges. Pierce all over with fork. Bake until golden brown, about 11 minutes. Cool slightly on rack. Reduce oven to 375°F.

Spread preserves in bottom of crust. Top with almonds. Arrange apricots cut side down atop almonds, filling tart completely. Sprinkle with sugar. Dot apricots with butter. Bake until apricots are tender and filling is syrupy, about 1 hour. Cool on rack.

A LITTLE BITE MUSIC

IF IT'S TIME TO SET THE MOOD FOR A meal, you're better off opting for kinder, gentler melodies, according to researchers at Johns Hopkins University. They found that people not only relaxed their eating pace when a meal was accompanied by slow, soothing music, such as a flute instrumental, but also left food on their plates and suffered less from indigestion. In contrast, those who dined while listening to lively, high-spirited tunes took more bites per minute and ate more. An article in the *Tufts University Diet & Nutrition Letter* also mentioned that those doing the easy listening passed on second helpings—a high note for dieters.

PEACH TART WITH ALMOND CRUST

8 SERVINGS

CRUST

1 cup sliced almonds (about 4 ounces)

1 cup all-purpose flour

½ cup sugar

½ cup chilled unsalted butter, cut into pieces

1 egg yolk, beaten to blend

½ teaspoon vanilla extract

FILLING

2 tablespoons peach preserves

¼ cup sliced almonds, finely chopped

1½ pounds ripe peaches, peeled, pitted, cut into ½-inch-thick slices

3 tablespoons sugar

1½ teaspoons grated lemon peel

2 tablespoons (¼ stick) unsalted butter

Additional sliced almonds

Vanilla ice cream or mascarpone cheese

FOR CRUST: Butter 9-inch-diameter tart pan with removable bottom. Coarsely grind almonds in processor. Add flour and sugar and continue processing until nuts are finely ground. Add butter and process using on/off turns until mixture resembles coarse meal. Pour egg yolk and vanilla over flour mixture and process using on/off turns until mixture forms large moist clumps. Press enough dough onto bottom and up sides of tart pan to form ¼-inch-thick crust. (Reserve any remaining dough for another use.) Refrigerate crust until well chilled, about 30 minutes. (*Can be prepared 1 day ahead. Cover tightly with plastic wrap and refrigerate.*)

Preheat oven to 375°F. Bake crust until golden brown, about 20 minutes. Cool crust completely on rack. Maintain oven temperature.

FOR FILLING: Spread preserves evenly over bottom of crust. Sprinkle ¼ cup almonds over preserves. Arrange sliced peaches atop almonds in slightly overlapping spiral pattern. Sprinkle peaches with sugar and lemon peel. Dot top of tart with butter. Sprinkle with additional almonds. Bake until peaches are tender, about 35 minutes. Cool slightly. Serve warm or at room temperature with vanilla ice cream or mascarpone cheese.

MACADAMIA LIME PIE

The delicious macadamia nut crust is an innovative twist on a favorite dessert. Use Florida Key limes if possible.

8 SERVINGS

1 3½-ounce jar roasted macadamia nuts, rinsed, dried

1 cup fine vanilla wafer cookie crumbs (about 26 cookies)

1 tablespoon sugar

¼ cup (½ stick) butter, melted

½ cup plus 2 tablespoons fresh lime juice

1 teaspoon unflavored gelatin
3 egg yolks
1 14-ounce can sweetened condensed milk
1 teaspoon grated lime peel
1 cup chilled whipping cream, whipped to stiff peaks

Preheat oven to 350°F. Place nuts on cookie sheet and toast until golden brown, stirring several times and watching carefully, about 2 minutes. Remove from oven. Cool completely. Maintain oven temperature. Grind ½ cup macadamia nuts in processor. Transfer nuts to medium bowl. Add cookie crumbs, sugar and butter and mix. Press mixture into 9-inch pie pan. Bake until golden brown, about 10 minutes. Cool.

Place 2 tablespoons lime juice in small bowl. Sprinkle gelatin over and let stand until softened, about 10 minutes. Meanwhile, whisk egg yolks and condensed milk in heavy medium saucepan to blend. Whisk in remaining ½ cup lime juice. Stir over medium heat 6 minutes to cook eggs (do not boil). Add softened gelatin and lime peel and stir until gelatin dissolves. Pour filling into prepared crust and refrigerate until filling is set, about 6 hours or overnight.

Spread whipped cream decoratively over pie. Chop remaining macadamia nuts and sprinkle over cream. Cut into wedges and serve.

Save the leftovers for dessert tomorrow night.

LEMON, HONEY AND WALNUT TART

6 TO 8 SERVINGS

CRUST

½ cup (1 stick) unsalted butter, room temperature
⅓ cup sugar
1 large egg yolk
½ teaspoon vanilla extract
¼ teaspoon salt
⅛ teaspoon ground cloves
1⅓ cups all-purpose flour

FILLING

½ cup sugar
⅓ cup honey
¼ cup fresh lemon juice
3 large eggs
1½ tablespoons grated lemon peel
¾ teaspoon baking powder
¼ teaspoon ground cloves
Pinch of salt
1 cup chopped walnuts (about 4 ounces)

Powdered sugar
Halved strawberries

FOR CRUST: Mix first 6 ingredients with electric mixer until well blended. Add flour and mix until just combined. Gather dough into ball; flatten to disk. Wrap in plastic and refrigerate at least 1 hour. (*Can be prepared 1 day ahead. Let dough soften slightly before continuing.*)

Preheat oven to 350°F. Butter and flour 9-inch-diameter tart pan with removable bottom. Roll dough out between sheets of waxed paper to 12-

inch-diameter round. Remove top sheet. Transfer dough to prepared pan, discarding second sheet. Trim and finish edges. Refrigerate 15 minutes.

Line dough with foil and fill with dried beans or pie weights. Bake 15 minutes. Remove beans and foil and continue baking until crust is golden brown, about 15 minutes. Cool completely on rack. (Can be prepared 1 day ahead. Let stand at room temperature.)

FOR FILLING: Preheat oven to 350°F. Mix first 8 ingredients in bowl until smooth. Spread walnuts in crust. Pour lemon mixture over. Bake until filling is just set in center; about 35 minutes.

Cool tart on rack. Sprinkle with powdered sugar. Arrange strawberry halves, points towards center, around outer edge of tart and serve

PASSOVER FRUIT TART

This tart is a new twist on the centuries-old honey-nut-spice combination typical of European Jewish cooking. There is enough pastry to make two dozen crisp spice cookies in addition to the tart crust.

8 SERVINGS

1½ cups firmly packed light brown sugar
1 cup (2 sticks) unsalted margarine, room temperature
2 tablespoons solid vegetable shortening
⅓ cup almond paste (about 3 ounces), crumbled into small pieces
1 egg
½ cup honey
1 tablespoon kosher Concord grape wine
1 tablespoon cinnamon
1 teaspoon ground ginger
¼ teaspoon salt
3½ cups matzo meal

½ cup potato starch
1½ cups (about) almonds, lightly toasted and ground
½ cup raspberry preserves
½ cup apricot preserves
2 tablespoons kosher Concord grape wine
Fresh fruit, such as strawberries, raspberries, kiwi, grapes, plum and peach slices

In large bowl, beat brown sugar, margarine, shortening and almond paste until fluffy. Beat in egg. Add honey. Stir in matzo meal and potato starch. Divide dough into thirds; flatten into disks. Wrap separately in plastic and chill until firm, about 2 hours. (*Can be prepared 1 day ahead.*)

Preheat oven to 350°F. Sprinkle work surface with ¼ cup ground almonds. Place 1 dough piece atop nuts and sprinkle more almonds over. Roll ut to ¼-inch-thick round, using ...onds as necessary to prevent ...ing. Roll dough up on rolling pin and transfer to 9-inch-diameter tart pan with removable bottom. Trim and crimp edges. Spread raspberry preserves evenly in pastry. Bake until crust is golden brown, about 30 minutes. Cool tart on wire rack.

Meanwhile, lightly grease 2 large cookie sheets. Sprinkle work surface with ¼ cup ground almonds. Place dough piece atop nuts and sprinkle with more ground almonds. Roll out dough to thickness of ¼ inch, using more almonds as necessary to prevent sticking. Cut out 2-inch Stars of David and other shapes using cookie cutters. Transfer cookies to prepared cookie sheets. Bake until golden brown, about 15 minutes. Transfer to rack and cool. Repeat with remaining dough piece and ground almonds. (*Tart and cookies can be prepared 1 day ahead. Cover and store at room temperature.*)

Melt apricot preserves with 2 tablespoons wine in small saucepan over medium heat. Strain into small bowl and cool slightly. Arrange fruit decoratively atop raspberry preserves. Brush tart with apricot glaze. Place 4 or 5 cookie stars decoratively atop tart. (*Fruit can be prepared 6 hours ahead.*) Cut tart into wedges and serve. Pass cookies separately. (*Store remaining spice cookies in airtight container.*)

FRESH FRUIT TART WITH BOYSENBERRY CREAM

Any colorful combination of seasonal fruit can be used to decorate this pretty dessert. The boysenberry filling is an American take on the usual vanilla cream.

8 SERVINGS

FILLING
1 large egg
2 large egg yolks
1 tablespoon cornstarch
2 teaspoons fresh lemon juice
1 ½-pint basket fresh boysenberries or 1⅓ cups frozen unsweetened boysenberries, thawed
½ cup sugar
¼ cup (½ stick) unsalted butter

CRUST
1¼ cups unbleached all-purpose flour
¼ cup sugar
Pinch of salt
7 tablespoons cold unsalted butter, cut into small pieces
1 teaspoon grated lemon peel (yellow part only)
3 tablespoons fresh lemon juice

1 1-pint basket strawberries, stemmed, halved
1 ½-pint basket fresh raspberries
1 ½-pint basket fresh boysenberries or blackberries
1 large peach, cut into ½-inch-wide slices
5 tablespoons currant jelly

FOR FILLING: Beat egg and yolks in small

bowl to blend. Dissolve cornstarch in lemon juice in small bowl. Mix into eggs. Puree berries and sugar in blender. Strain puree through fine sieve into medium saucepan. Add butter and bring to simmer over medium-high heat. Slowly whisk hot berry mixture into egg mixture. Return mixture to same saucepan and cook until filling is very thick and boils, whisking constantly, about 3 minutes. Transfer filling to small bowl. Press plastic wrap directly onto surface to prevent skin from forming; refrigerate at least 6 hours. (*Can be prepared 1 day ahead.*)

FOR CRUST: Blend flour, sugar and salt in processor. Add butter and lemon peel and process using on/off turns until coarse meal forms. Add lemon juice and process until moist clumps form. Gather into ball; flatten into disk. Wrap dough in plastic and refrigerate 45 minutes. (*Can be prepared 1 day ahead. Let soften slightly at room temperature before continuing.*)

Position rack in center of oven and preheat to 350°F. Roll dough cut on lightly floured surface to ⅛-inch-thick round. Fold dough over rolling pin and transfer to 9x1-inch tart pan with removable bottom. Gently press dough into pan. Trim and finish edges. Chill 15 minutes. Line dough with foil and fill with dry beans or pie weights. Bake 15 minutes. Remove beans and foil and bake until crust is golden, about 20 minutes longer. Transfer crust to rack and cool.

Spread filling evenly in crust. Arrange strawberries, cut side down, in irregular pattern on filling. Fill in with raspberries and boysenberries. Tuck peach slices between berries. Stir currant jelly in heavy small saucepan over low heat until melted. Brush jelly over fruit to glaze. (*Can be prepared 3 hours ahead. Refrigerate.*)

A Better Decaf

DECAFFEINATED COFFEES FROM SWISS Water offer rich, full flavor and, unlike brands that use chemicals, employ only water and carbon filters to decaffeinate their beans. Ask about the Swiss Water collection at your local coffee store or, for a supplier near you, write to Coffex North America, P.O. Box 2170, Vancouver, B.C. V6B 3V6, Canada.

PUFF PASTRY BASKETS WITH HONEY MOUSSE AND ASSORTED FRUIT

Custard-filled pastry horns are a specialty of Navarre. We've fashioned our pastry into basket shapes and filled them with a honey mousse. This recipe makes eight baskets, so serve the six prettiest.

6 SERVINGS

SAUCE

2 large ripe mangoes, peeled, pitted, sliced
2 tablespoons honey
⅓ cup (about) mango nectar

MOUSSE

1 tablespoon water
1 teaspoon unflavored gelatin
¼ cup honey
4 egg yolks
⅔ cup chilled whipping cream
⅓ cup chilled crème fraîche or sour cream

PASTRIES

3 tablespoons sugar
¼ teaspoon (generous) ground allspice
1 17¼-ounce package (2 sheets) frozen puff pastry, thawed

½ pineapple, peeled, cored, sliced
1 mango, halved, peeled, sliced
2 kiwi fruits, peeled, sliced
Fresh mint leaves

FOR SAUCE: Puree 2 mangoes and 2 tablespoons honey in processor. Cover and refrigerate until well chilled, about 1 hour. Add mango nectar as needed to thin to sauce consistency. (*Sauce can be made 1 day ahead. Keep refrigerated.*)

FOR MOUSSE: Place 1 tablespoon water in ¼-cup measuring cup. Sprinkle gelatin over. Let soften 10 minutes. Whisk honey and yolks in small metal bowl. Set bowl over large saucepan halfway filled with boiling water. Cook until mixture registers 160°F on candy ther-

mometer; whisking constantly, about 3 minutes. Remove bowl from over water. Add gelatin mixture and whisk until honey mixture is cool.

Beat whipping cream and crème fraîche in large bowl to medium-stiff peaks. Add honey mixture and fold together gently. Cover and refrigerate mousse until set, at least 2 hours and up to 8 hours.

FOR PASTRIES: Preheat oven to 375°F. Combine sugar and ground allspice in small bowl. Sprinkle 1 tablespoon sugar mixture over 1 puff pastry sheet. Roll out on lightly floured surface to 13x12-inch rectangle. Trim to 10-inch square. Cut puff pastry sheet into quarters, forming four 5-inch squares. Fold 1 dough square diagonally in half to form triangle. Starting at folded side, cut ½-inch border strip on both unfolded sides of triangle, leaving ½ inch of dough uncut at triangle point so that strips remain attached. Unfold triangle. Brush ½-inch-wide border strips with water. Lift up both loose corner tips, slip one under the other and place border strips atop edges of base, gently pulling to match corners on base. Press border onto base to adhere. Sprinkle more sugar mixture over border. Transfer pastry to cookie sheet. Pierce center all over with fork. Repeat with remaining pastry squares and pastry sheet and sugar mixture. Bake pastries until golden brown, piercing centers with knife if puffy, about 20 minutes. Transfer pastries to rack and cool completely. (*Can be prepared 4 hours ahead. Store in airtight container at room temperature.*)

Spoon sauce onto plates. Spoon honey mousse into pastry baskets and arrange atop sauce. Top mousse with slices of pineapple, mango and kiwi fruit. Garnish each dessert with fresh mint leaves and serve.

PHYLLO PURSES WITH RASPBERRY SAUCE

These pastry bundles filled with apples and nuts are presented with a tangy raspberry sauce. Champagne makes a natural go-with. After dessert, pass chocolate truffles to enjoy with espresso.

10 SERVINGS

3 tablespoons unsalted butter
2 pounds Granny Smith apples, peeled, cored, chopped
¼ cup sugar
¼ cup Grand Marnier or other orange liqueur
½ cup finely chopped toasted walnuts
½ cup finely chopped toasted almonds
¼ cup chopped toasted pistachios
3 tablespoons honey
1½ teaspoons fresh lemon juice
10 frozen phyllo pastry sheets, thawed

¾ cup (1½ sticks) unsalted butter, melted
15 teaspoons sugar
Powdered sugar
Raspberry Sauce (see recipe)

Melt 3 tablespoons unsalted butter in heavy large skillet over medium-high heat. Add chopped apples. Sprinkle with ¼ cup sugar. Cook until apples are golden brown, stirring occasionally, 8 minutes. Mix in Grand Marnier. Cool. Stir in walnuts, almonds, pistachios, honey and fresh lemon juice. (*Filling can be prepared 4 hours ahead. Cover and let stand at room temperature.*)

Preheat oven to 375°F. Butter heavy large cookie sheet. Place 1 phyllo sheet on work surface. Brush lightly with melted butter. Sprinkle with ½ teaspoon sugar. Fold pastry in half crosswise. Brush lightly with melted butter and sprinkle with ½ teaspoon sugar. Fold crosswise in half again. Brush lightly with melted butter and sprinkle with ½ teaspoon sugar. Mound ¼ cup apple filling in center of pastry. Gather up pastry sides and twist at center to seal, forming purse shape. Place on prepared cookie sheet. Brush pastry with melted butter. Repeat with remaining pastry, melted butter, sugar and filling, forming total of 10 packages.

Bake pastries until golden brown, about 25 minutes. (*Can be prepared 4 hours ahead. Let stand at room temperature.*) Sift powdered sugar over pastries. Spoon raspberry sauce onto plates. Place warm or room-temperature pastries on sauce and serve.

RASPBERRY SAUCE

MAKES ABOUT 2½ CUPS

2 12-ounce bags frozen unsweetened raspberries, thawed
6 tablespoons powdered sugar

Puree raspberries and sugar in processor. Strain to remove seeds. Cover and refrigerate until well chilled. (*Can be prepared 1 day ahead.*)

PHYLLO EASTER BASKETS WITH LEMON CURD AND STRAWBERRIES

Crisp pastry baskets filled with zesty lemon curd and fresh strawberries. The pastry is placed in every other cup of the buttered muffin tins because the pastry corners will expand during baking. All the components can be prepared ahead, leaving just a quick final assembly.

MAKES 12 BASKETS

4 frozen phyllo dough sheets, thawed
¼ cup (½ stick) unsalted butter, melted
6 teaspoons dry white breadcrumbs

LEMON CURD

1 cup sugar
3 large eggs
1 egg yolk
½ cup (1 stick) unsalted butter, cut into pieces
6 tablespoons fresh lemon juice
2 tablespoons grated lemon peel

1 1-pint basket strawberries, hulled and sliced
Fresh mint sprigs

FOR BASKETS: Preheat oven to 350°F. Place 1 phyllo sheet on work surface. Brush with butter. Sprinkle 2 teaspoons breadcrumbs over Top with second phyllo sheet. Brush with butter. Sprinkle 2 teaspoons breadcrumbs over Top with third phyllo sheet. Brush with butter. Sprinkle remaining breadcrumbs over Top with fourth phyllo sheet. Brush with butter. Cut out twelve 4-inch squares from phyllo. Brush every other cup of two twelve ½-cup muffin tins with melted butter. Place 1 phyllo square in each buttered cup, pressing pastry down in center and around edges to mold to cup (pastry corners should stick up). Bake until just golden brown and crisp, about 10 minutes. Remove pastry from tins and cool completely. *(Pastry baskets can be prepared 2 days ahead. Store in single layer in airtight container.)*

FOR CURD: Whisk first 6 ingredients in heavy medium saucepan over low heat until butter melts. Cook until mixture thickens to consistency of lightly whipped cream, whisking constantly, about 5 minutes. Pour into bowl. Cover and refrigerate until cold, about 4 hours. *(Can be prepared 2 days ahead.)*

Spoon some berries into bottom of each phyllo basket. Top each with 2½ tablespoons lemon curd. Arrange remaining berries in petal fashion atop curd. Garnish with mint sprigs.

Convenience Items: Baking Made Easier

Frozen Puff Pastry: What's available is almost as good as homemade—quite a boon, considering that the homemade can take hours to prepare. Keep a box in the freezer, and thaw the pastry sheets at room temperature or in the refrigerator, according to package directions, as you need them.

Frozen Phyllo Dough: Since very few bakers have either the time, inclination or skill necessary to prepare phyllo, the store-bought version makes elaborate strudels and baklava not only simple but doable. Keep a package on hand in the freezer.

Prepared Pie Crusts: There are several different kinds of pie crusts available, beginning with the frozen crusts in foil pie pans familiar to most everyone. These come in regular and deep-dish versions. A newer refrigerated pie crust is available in the dairy case. Look for a box containing two pastry sheets, folded in quarters. And in the baking aisle, you'll find graham cracker crusts in foil pans; neither refrigeration nor baking is required for them.

Quick Fix-its

Egg Whites That Won't Thicken: The presence of any fat or water will prevent egg whites from thickening when beaten. To avoid this, make sure there is no yolk in the whites and that the bowl and beaters are completely dry and clean.

Cures for Dry, Heavy and/or Burned Cakes: A cake will turn out dry if it is baked at too high a temperature or for too long a time. Soak the cake with fruit syrup, rum or brandy, or use it for cake crumbs or in a trifle. A heavy cake is usually the result of overbeating or baking at too low a temperature. While you can't fix it, you can learn from your mistakes. If you burn the top of a cake, you can trim it, making sure to remove all the bitter dark areas.

Saving Overwhipped Cream: If you overwhip cream, gently fold in some unwhipped cream a little at a time. This will thin it, and though the resulting cream will be dense rather than light, it will be usable.

Cream That Won't Whip: This can happen if the cream, beaters, bowl or even room are too warm, or if the sugar or flavoring is added too soon. Always begin with well-chilled cream; you can also chill the bowl and beaters in the refrigerator. Add sugar and flavorings after the cream has begun to thicken.

Patching Pie Shells: Occasionally, a pie or tart shell will develop a hole or split during prebaking. If you've saved your dough trimmings, and if the pie is going to be filled and baked further, the hole or tear can be patched. Roll out a thin piece of uncooked dough, brush it with water and gently press it over the hole or crack. Then continue with the recipe.

Tricks of the Trade

Folding: To fold together two ingredients, such as whipped cream into a custard, first stir a spoonful of the cream into the custard to lighten it, then turn that mixture into the whipped cream. Using a rubber spatula, cut straight down through the center of the mixture then turn the spatula toward you and lift up. Turn the bowl an inch or two and repeat. Continue the folding procedure, working quickly around the bowl, just until no streaks remain.

Beating Egg Whites: Begin with a clean bowl and beaters, and room-temperature egg whites without a trace of yolk in them. Beat at medium-slow speed until foaming, about 2 minutes. Add salt, cream of tartar and/or sugar (stabilizing ingredients) as the recipe directs and beat, gradually increasing the speed, until stiff and shiny peaks form.

Rolling Out and Lifting Pastry: Using your hand, press the dough flat on a smooth, lightly floured surface. Lightly flour the rolling pin and roll out the dough in short, even strokes, working from the center out. Carefully fold the pastry over the rolling pin, lift gently and drape it over the pan.

Prebaking Pastry: Prebaking pastry before filling helps prevent the crust from becoming soggy. After fitting the pastry into the pan, line it with a sheet of parchment paper or aluminum foil. Fill with dried beans or pie weights. Bake at 450°F for about 15 minutes. Remove beans and paper; prick the bottom with a fork and continue baking until the crust is just beginning to color and pull away from the sides of the pan, a few minutes more. Cool before filling.

Frozen Desserts

What could be a more refreshing way to end a meal than to serve up a glistening scoop of Pink Grapefruit Champagne Sorbet, creamy Mango-Macadamia Nut Ice Cream, Coffee and Orange Granita Suprema or Margarita Sherbet with Candied Lime Peel? Frozen desserts are a breeze to prepare, and their vivid colors and lively flavors make them a memorable way to conclude a gala evening.

SUNSET SORBET SUNDAES

Colorful boysenberry and mango sorbets team up in a refreshing, guilt-free alternative to traditional ice cream sundaes.

6 SERVINGS

1 16-ounce bag frozen unsweetened boysenberries or blackberries, thawed

½ cup plus 6 tablespoons sugar

½ cup light corn syrup

¼ cup water

¼ cup crème de cassis (optional)

2 large mangoes, peeled, pitted

1 mango, peeled, pitted, sliced

1 1-pint basket fresh boysenberries or blackberries

Combine thawed boysenberries, ½ cup sugar, ¼ cup corn syrup, ¼ cup water and crème de cassis in heavy medium saucepan. Bring to simmer, stirring frequently. Puree in processor. Strain into medium bowl, pressing on solids with spoon. Pour ¾ cup puree into small bowl; cover and refrigerate to use later as sauce. Refrigerate remaining berry puree in medium bowl until cold. Transfer puree in medium bowl to ice cream maker and process according to manufacturer's instructions. Transfer sorbet to container and freeze.

Puree 2 mangoes in processor. Measure puree and return 1⅔ cups to processor. Reserve any remaining puree for another use. Add remaining 6 tablespoons sugar and remaining ¼ cup corn syrup to processor; blend well. Transfer mango puree to ice cream maker and freeze according to manufacturer's instructions. Transfer sorbet to container and freeze. *(Sauce and sorbets can be prepared 2 days ahead.)*

Scoop sorbets into parfait dishes or onto plates. Garnish with sliced mango and berries. Spoon sauce over.

MARGARITA SHERBET WITH CANDIED LIME PEEL

A dessert version of the famous Mexican cocktail. We even coat the rims of the glasses with sugar to mimic the drink.

6 TO 8 SERVINGS

PEEL

3 to 4 fresh limes
¼ cup sugar
3 tablespoons water

SHERBET

¾ cup fresh lime juice (about 10 limes)
1 cup sugar
2 cups cold lowfat milk
Sugar (for rims of glasses)
6 tablespoons tequila
6 tablespoons triple sec
6 thin lime slices

FOR PEEL: Using vegetable peeler, remove peel (green part only) from limes in strips. Cut enough peel into very thin strips to measure ¾ cup. Combine peel with enough cold water to cover by 1 inch in small saucepan. Bring to boil. Cover and simmer peel 5 minutes. Drain and rinse peel.

Stir ¼ cup sugar and 3 tablespoons water in small saucepan over medium-low heat until sugar dissolves. Bring syrup to boil. Cover and cook 1 minute. Uncover and simmer 1 minute longer. Add lime peel strips and simmer 1 minute. Transfer lime peel and syrup to bowl. Cover and refrigerate. (*Can be prepared 3 days ahead.*)

FOR SHERBET: Stir lime juice and 1 cup sugar together in medium bowl until sugar dissolves. Mix in cold lowfat milk (mixture may look curdled but will become smooth during freezing). Transfer to ice cream maker and process according to manufacturer's instructions. When sherbet is almost set, use fork to lift half of candied lime peel from syrup and add peel to sherbet. Process sherbet until set. Transfer sherbet to container. Cover and freeze 2 hours. (*Sherbet can be prepared 1 day ahead. Keep covered and frozen.*)

Moisten rims of Margarita glasses. Dip rims in sugar to coat well. Scoop sherbet into glasses. Drizzle each with 1 tablespoon tequila and 1 tablespoon triple sec. Garnish sherbet with lime slice and some of remaining candied lime peel and serve.

PINK GRAPEFRUIT CHAMPAGNE SORBET WITH PINK GRAPEFRUIT SAUCE

A pretty pale pink sorbet enhanced with a splash of champagne.

6 SERVINGS

5 cups fresh pink grapefruit juice (from about 6 large grapefruits)
1¼ cups sugar
¼ cup light corn syrup
1 tablespoon grated pink grapefruit peel

¾ cup champagne or other sparkling wine

2 pink grapefruits (optional)

Fresh mint sprigs

Stir first 4 ingredients in large saucepan over medium heat just until sugar dissolves. Strain into bowl, pressing on solids; mix in champagne Pour 2 cups juice mixture into medium saucepan. Refrigerate remaining juice mixture in bowl. Simmer mixture in saucepan until reduced to ¾ cup, stirring occasionally, about 25 minutes. Refrigerate reduced mixture to use as sauce Transfer juice mixture in bowl to ice cream maker and freeze according to manufacturer's instructions. Transfer sorbet to container; cover and freeze (*Sauce and sorbet can be prepared 3 days ahead.*)

Cut peel and white pith from grapefruits. Working over bowl, cut between membranes to release segments. (*Can be prepared 6 hours ahead. Place segments in bowl with juice. Cover and refrigerate.*)

Chill 6 plates in freezer. Scoop 3 ovals of sorbet onto each plate. Spoon sauce around sorbet. Decorate with grapefruit segments. Garnish with mint.

COFFEE AND ORANGE GRANITA SUPREMA

You don't need an ice cream maker to prepare this classic frozen treat, which includes only 2 tablespoons of cream per serving. Accompany with amaretti or other Italian cookies.

6 SERVINGS

4 cups hot espresso or strong coffee made with ground espresso coffee beans

½ cup sugar

1 teaspoon grated orange peel

⅛ teaspoon ground cinnamon

¾ cup well-chilled whipping cream

3 tablespoons sugar

2 tablespoons Grand Marnier or other orange liqueur

Milk chocolate curls

Thin orange peel strips

Mix coffee, ½ cup sugar, grated orange peel and ground cinnamon in medium bowl until sugar dissolves. Cool to room temperature. Transfer mixture to loaf pan. Freeze until granita is consistency of shaved ice, stirring mixture with fork and breaking up frozen edge pieces every 30 minutes, about 3 hours. (*Granita can be made 6 hours ahead. If possible, stir every 30 minutes to 1 hour. Before serving, blend mixture in processor to break up ice.*)

Beat chilled whipping cream and 3 tablespoons sugar in medium bowl until soft peaks form. Add Grand Marnier and beat until soft peaks form again. Spoon granita into bowls. Top each dessert with dollop of whipped cream. Garnish with chocolate curls and orange peel strips and serve immediately.

LEMON SORBET WITH FRESH BLUEBERRIES AND BLUEBERRY SAUCE

8 SERVINGS

SAUCE

4 cups fresh blueberries or
  1 pound frozen, thawed
1 cup water
3 tablespoons fresh lemon juice
2 tablespoons cornstarch
3 tablespoons sugar

3 half-pints lemon sorbet or sherbet
2 cups fresh blueberries
  Thinly sliced lemon peel (yellow
    part only)
  Fresh lemon balm or mint sprigs

FOR SAUCE: Combine first 4 ingredients in heavy large saucepan. Stir over medium-high heat until mixture boils and thickens. Cool slightly. Puree mixture in processor or blender until smooth. Mix in sugar. Refrigerate until chilled, about 3 hours. (*Can be prepared 2 days ahead.*)

Scoop sorbet into goblets. Spoon sauce over. Top with fresh berries. Garnish with lemon peel and lemon balm.

MANGO-MACADAMIA NUT ICE CREAM

Be sure to use extra-ripe mangoes when preparing this rich, creamy dessert.

MAKES ABOUT 5 CUPS

2 cups whipping cream
1 cup milk (do not use lowfat
    or nonfat)
6 egg yolks
1 cup sugar
2 large ripe mangoes (about
    22 ounces), peeled, pitted, diced
2 teaspoons fresh lime juice
½ teaspoon grated lime peel
1 cup unsalted macadamia nuts,
    toasted, coarsely chopped

Bring 2 cups whipping cream and 1 cup milk to boil in heavy large saucepan. Whisk yolks and sugar to blend in medium bowl. Gradually whisk hot cream into yolk mixture. Return to same saucepan. Stir over low heat until custard thickens and leaves path on back of spoon when finger is drawn across, about 5 minutes. Immediately transfer custard to blender. Add mangoes and blend until smooth. Chill custard. Stir in remaining ingredients. Process in ice cream maker according to manufacturer's instructions. Freeze ice cream in covered container. (*Can be prepared 2 days ahead.*)

Lemon Meringue Terrine

The combination of lemon and almond flavors is irresistible in this frozen dessert.

12 SERVINGS

TOASTED ALMOND MERINGUES

Powdered sugar
5 large egg whites, room temperature
½ teaspoon cream of tartar
1 cup sugar
½ teaspoon vanilla extract
¼ teaspoon almond extract
1¼ cups ground toasted blanched almonds (about 6 ounces)
1 tablespoon cornstarch

LEMON MOUSSE

4 large eggs
1 cup sugar
½ cup fresh lemon juice
½ cup whipping cream
2 tablespoons grated lemon peel
1¼ cups chilled whipping cream
1 teaspoon vanilla extract

1½ cups toasted sliced almonds

FOR MERINGUES: Preheat oven to 275°F. Line 2 large cookie sheets with foil. Butter foil and dust with powdered sugar. Cut a 12x4-inch cardboard rectangle. Using cardboard as guide, trace 2 rectangles on each prepared cookie sheet.

Using electric mixer, beat egg whites and cream of tartar in large bowl until soft peaks form. Gradually add sugar and beat until stiff and shiny. Beat in vanilla and almond extracts. Combine almonds and cornstarch in medium bowl. Gently fold nuts into egg whites in 2 additions. Spread 1¼ cups meringue over each marked rectangle on prepared sheets, filling rectangles completely. Bake until meringues are crisp and golden, about 1 hour. Cool meringues on sheets. Remove carefully and trim to 12x4 inches if necessary. *(Can be prepared 2 days ahead. Wrap tightly and store at room temperature.)*

FOR MOUSSE: Whisk eggs and sugar in large bowl until thick. Whisk in lemon juice. Scald ½ cup cream in heavy medium saucepan. Gradually whisk hot cream into egg mixture. Return mixture to saucepan and stir over medium heat until mixture thickens and leaves path on back of spoon when finger is drawn across, about 4 minutes. Do not boil. Pour into large bowl; mix in lemon peel. Press plastic onto surface of custard and refrigerate until cold, about 1 hour. Whip 1¼ cups chilled cream and vanilla extract in large bowl until firm peaks form. Fold cream into lemon mixture in 2 additions.

Place 1 meringue on platter. Spread with 1 generous cup mousse. Top with second meringue. Spread with 1 generous cup mousse. Top with third meringue. Spread with 1 generous cup mousse. Top with last meringue. Frost top and sides with remaining mousse. Press sliced almonds gently into mousse over top and sides of terrine. Freeze at least 4 hours. *(Can be prepared 4 days ahead. Wrap* carefully. Keep frozen.) Let stand at room temperature 15 minutes before serving.

CAVA, STRAWBERRY AND ORANGE SORBET

Ninety-nine percent of cava—Spanish sparkling wine—is made in Catalonia. So it's natural that the bubbly beverage has found its way into many elegant Catalan desserts. Here we combine it with the luscious flavors and bright colors of strawberries and oranges in a refreshing sorbet.

8 SERVINGS

½ cup sugar
¼ cup water
1 10-ounce package frozen sweetened strawberries, thawed
1 cup orange juice
1 cup brut cava (Spanish sparkling wine)

Fresh strawberries

Stir sugar and water in small saucepan over medium-low heat until sugar dissolves. Bring to boil. Transfer to large bowl. Puree strawberries in processor. Add to syrup. Mix in orange juice and cava. Refrigerate strawberry mixture until well chilled.

Process strawberry mixture in ice cream maker according to manufacturer's instructions. Transfer sorbet to covered container and freeze until ready to serve. (Can be prepared 4 days ahead.)

Scoop sorbet into glasses. Top with fresh berries and serve.

PINEAPPLE WITH CITRUS SORBET AND STRAWBERRIES

6 SERVINGS

6 ½-inch-thick trimmed cored fresh pineapple slices
2 tablespoons sugar
3 tablespoons fresh lime juice
2 tablespoons light rum (optional)

Pineapple or lemon sorbet

2 1-pint baskets fresh strawberries, hulled, sliced
2 pints lemon or lime sorbet
Fresh mint leaves

Place pineapple in large dish. Sprinkle with sugar. Drizzle with lime juice and rum. Cover and chill 1 to 6 hours.

Arrange 1 pineapple ring on each plate. Place strawberries in bowl. Pour any pineapple juices from dish over berries and toss gently. Arrange strawberries in star-burst pattern around pineapple. Place scoop of sorbet in center of ring. Garnish with mint.

SORBET WITH VODKA-MARINATED PLUMS

2 SERVINGS
CAN BE DOUBLED OR TRIPLED

2 plums, sliced
¼ cup chilled vodka
2 tablespoons sugar
½ teaspoon grated lemon peel

Pineapple or lemon sorbet

Combine first 4 ingredients in bowl. Stir until sugar dissolves. Refrigerate plum mixture at least 20 minutes.

Spoon sorbet into balloon glasses. Top with plums and marinating liquid.

Pureed Peach and Raspberry Coupes
(COVER RECIPE)

A touch of fruit vinegar in the puree brings out its flavor and helps preserve the color.

4 SERVINGS

1 pound ripe peaches, peeled, pitted
3 tablespoons peach brandy or peach nectar
1½ tablespoons (about) sugar
2 teaspoons raspberry vinegar or other fruit vinegar

1 pint vanilla frozen yogurt
1 cup fresh raspberries

Puree peaches, brandy, 1½ tablespoons sugar and vinegar in processor until smooth. Let stand 5 minutes. Process 1 minute longer, adding more sugar if desired. Transfer puree to small bowl. Cover and refrigerate at least 15 minutes. (*Can be prepared 3 hours ahead.*)

Spoon puree into 4 shallow dishes. Top with scoops of frozen yogurt. Sprinkle with raspberries and serve.

Frozen Strawberry-Banana Cake with Strawberry Sauce

Purchased sorbet, frozen yogurt and pound cake make this a quick, elegant dessert.

12 SERVINGS

1 12-ounce pound cake
1 cup strawberry preserves
¼ cup strawberry liqueur or orange juice
2 pints strawberry sorbet, softened
2 pints banana-strawberry frozen yogurt, softened
1 10-ounce package frozen sliced strawberries in syrup, thawed
3 large ripe bananas, peeled, cut diagonally into ¼-inch-thick slices
Sliced fresh strawberries

Cut cake into ¼-inch-thick slices. Arrange enough slices in bottom of 9-inch-diameter springform pan with 2¾-inch-high sides to just cover bottom, fitting tightly. Cook preserves and liqueur in heavy small saucepan over medium heat until reduced to ⅔ cup, stirring frequently, about 14 minutes. Spread half of preserves mixture over cake in pan. Freeze 10 minutes. Spoon sorbet over cake in pan; smooth top. Arrange more cake slices over to just cover sorbet. Spread remaining preserves mixture over cake. Freeze 10 minutes.

Spoon frozen yogurt over cake; smooth top. Cover and freeze overnight. (*Can be prepared 1 week ahead.*)

Puree thawed berries in processor. Cover and refrigerate until cold. (*Sauce can be prepared 2 days ahead.*)

Release pan sides from cake. Place banana slices around cake edge. Mound berries in center. Serve cake with sauce

FROZEN BOYSENBERRY AND WHITE CHOCOLATE PARFAIT

Begin preparing this delicious dessert at least one day ahead.

6 SERVINGS

PARFAIT

1 16-ounce bag frozen boysenberries or blackberries, thawed

¼ cup sugar

1 tablespoon crème de cassis or other berry-flavored liqueur

½ teaspoon fresh lemon juice

¾ cup sugar

¼ cup water

6 large egg yolks

3 ounces imported white chocolate (such as Lindt), chopped, melted

2 teaspoons vanilla extract

1⅓ cups chilled whipping cream

SAUCE

1 16-ounce bag frozen boysenberries or blackberries, thawed

¼ cup sugar

2 tablespoons crème de cassis or other berry-flavored liqueur

Fresh boysenberries, blackberries or strawberries

Fresh mint sprigs

FOR PARFAIT: Line 9x5-inch loaf pan with plastic wrap. Puree berries and ¼ cup sugar in blender until just smooth. Strain. Measure 1⅓ cups puree and place in heavy small saucepan. (Reserve any remaining puree for sauce.) Simmer 1⅓ cups puree over medium heat until reduced to scant 1 cup, stirring occasionally, about 8 minutes. Transfer to bowl and chill 30 minutes. Stir in cassis and lemon juice. Refrigerate reduced puree until ready to use.

Combine ¾ cup sugar, water and yolks in medium metal bowl. Set bowl over saucepan of simmering water. Using hand-held electric mixer, beat yolk mixture until it registers 140°F on candy thermometer, occasionally scraping down sides of bowl, about 5 minutes. Continue cooking 3 minutes, beating constantly. Remove from over water. Add warm melted chocolate and vanilla extract and beat until cool. Beat whipping cream in another large bowl to stiff peaks. Gently mix ¼ of whipped cream into chocolate mixture. Fold in remaining whipped cream.

Transfer 1⅓ cups chocolate mixture to medium bowl. Fold in reduced berry puree. Fill prepared loaf pan with ⅓ of remaining chocolate mixture. Cover with berry-chocolate mixture. Top with remaining chocolate mixture. Smooth top. Freeze parfait overnight. (*Can be prepared 2 days ahead.*)

FOR SAUCE: Puree frozen boysenberries, sugar and crème de cassis in blender or processor until smooth. Strain. Add any berry puree reserved from parfait.

Unmold frozen parfait. Peel off

plastic wrap. Slice into ½-inch-thick slices. Drizzle with sauce. Garnish with berries and fresh mint sprigs.

MOLASSES COOKIE BASKETS WITH LEMON SORBET AND GINGERED FRUIT

A great dessert for summer dinner parties.

6 SERVINGS

COOKIES

¼ cup (½ stick) unsalted butter
¼ cup sugar
¼ cup light unsulfured molasses
½ teaspoon grated lemon peel
½ teaspoon ground ginger
1 teaspoon vanilla extract
½ cup all-purpose flour, sifted

FRUIT

½ cup sugar
½ cup water
¼ cup minced crystallized ginger

1 1-pint basket strawberries, hulled, quartered
1 ½-pint basket blueberries
2 peaches, peeled, pitted, sliced

2 pints purchased lemon sorbet

FOR COOKIES: Preheat oven to 325°F. Butter 2 large nonstick cookie sheets. Bring first 5 ingredients to simmer in heavy small saucepan over medium heat, stirring constantly. Remove from heat. Whisk in vanilla, then flour. Cool cookie mixture 10 minutes.

Drop mixture by level tablespoonfuls onto cookie sheets, spacing 6 inches apart and forming 3 cookies on each sheet. Using buttered fingertips, press out each round to 4½-inch diameter.

Bake 1 sheet until cookies are deep brown, about 12 minutes. Cool cookies on sheet just until firm enough to lift without breaking, about 2 minutes. Working quickly, lift 1 cookie from sheet. Drape cookie top side up over inverted ¾-cup custard dish. Gently flatten cookie on dish bottom; crimp sides to form fluted cup. Repeat with remaining 2 cookies, returning cookie sheet to oven briefly if cookies harden. Repeat baking and molding process with remaining cookies. Cool. Gently remove cookies from dishes.

FOR FRUIT: Stir first 3 ingredients in heavy small saucepan over medium heat until sugar dissolves. Increase heat and boil 3 minutes. Refrigerate ginger syrup until cold. (*Cookies and syrup can be prepared 1 week ahead. Store cookies at room temperature in airtight container. Keep sauce refrigerated.*) Place fruit in bowl. Add half of ginger syrup and toss well.

Place 1 cookie on each of 6 plates. Fill each with 3 scoops of sorbet and spoon fruit and remaining syrup over.

Lemon Sorbet
on the Half Shell

White chocolate is spooned over scallop shells to form pretty containers for this refreshing dessert. The shells can be found at specialty foods stores.

6 SERVINGS

WHITE CHOCOLATE SHELLS

6 scallop shells (about 4x4 inches)
16 ounces imported white chocolate (such as Lindt or Tobler), chopped

LEMON SORBET

3 cups water
1½ cups sugar
1 cup fresh lemon juice
1 tablespoon grated lemon peel
2 egg whites, beaten to blend
Pinch of salt

Ginger Sauce (see recipe)
Fresh mint

FOR SHELLS: Cut 6 squares of foil about 1 inch larger than shells. Place 1 square of foil, shiny side up, on back of shell. Fold one edge of foil under at base of shell, covering base. Hold shell in hand. Beginning at base and pressing with thumbs, press foil into ridges of shell. Fold foil edges under shell, completely covering shell with foil. Repeat process with remaining shells and foil.

Melt white chocolate in top of double boiler over simmering water, stirring until smooth. Cool white chocolate until just warm to touch.

Meanwhile, line large cookie sheet with waxed paper. Line small rimmed cookie sheet with foil. Set wire rack atop foil-lined cookie sheet. Place 1 foil-covered shell atop rack, foil side up. Slowly spoon chocolate over shell to coat evenly. Carefully transfer shell, chocolate side up, to waxed-paper-lined sheet using spatula. Repeat process with remaining shells and chocolate. Refrigerate 30 minutes.

Remove chocolate drippings from foil-lined cookie sheet. Add drippings to remaining white chocolate. Melt over simmering water, stirring until smooth. Cool until just warm to touch.

Set wire rack atop foil-lined cookie sheet. Line another large cookie sheet with waxed paper. Carefully transfer 1 shell to rack. Slowly spoon chocolate over chocolate-coated shell to coat evenly, forming second layer. Carefully transfer shell to waxed-paper-lined sheet. Repeat with remaining shells and chocolate. Refrigerate until chocolate is hard, about 1 hour. (*White chocolate shells can be prepared 1 week ahead. Refrigerate in airtight container*)

FOR SORBET: Bring water and sugar to boil in heavy medium saucepan, stirring until sugar dissolves. Boil 5 minutes. Cool. Refrigerate syrup until well chilled, about 1 hour or overnight.

Stir lemon juice and lemon peel into syrup. Transfer mixture to ice cream maker. Process according to manufacturer's instructions until just beginning to freeze firmly. Stir egg whites and salt into lemon mixture and continue processing until sorbet is firm.

Transfer sorbet to covered container and freeze overnight. (*Sorbet can be prepared up to 1 week ahead.*)

Place paper towel in hand. Place 1 shell on paper towel chocolate side down. Carefully remove foil from shell. Carefully peel foil off chocolate. Unmold remaining shells. Refrigerate chocolate shells if necessary.

Place 1 shell, rounded side down, on each of 6 plates. Place 1 scoop sorbet in center of each shell. Top with Ginger Sauce. Garnish with mint and serve.

GINGER SAUCE

Try this on fruit or vanilla ice cream for an unusual taste treat.

MAKES ABOUT ⅔ CUP

½ cup ginger preserves
2 tablespoons fresh orange juice
1 tablespoon fresh lemon juice
½ teaspoon grated orange peel
⅛ teaspoon vanilla extract

Combine all ingredients in small bowl. Cover and refrigerate overnight to mellow flavors. (*Sauce can be prepared up to 4 days ahead.*)

VANILLA MERINGUES WITH PLUM SAUCE

Try scoops of raspberry sorbet or vanilla frozen yogurt as a cool filling for these light and airy summertime treats.

6 SERVINGS

MERINGUES

3 large egg whites, room temperature
½ teaspoon cream of tartar
Pinch of salt
1¼ teaspoons vanilla extract
¾ cup sugar

SAUCE

4 ripe plums, pitted, sliced
¼ cup sugar
2 tablespoons slivovitz (plum brandy) or other brandy
½ teaspoon grated lemon peel
1½ pints raspberry sorbet or vanilla frozen yogurt

FOR MERINGUES: Position rack in center of oven and preheat to 275°F. Using 3-inch-diameter cardboard round or 3-inch cookie cutter, trace 6 circles on parchment sheet, spacing evenly. Invert parchment onto baking sheet. Using electric mixer, beat whites in large bowl at medium speed until frothy. Add cream of tartar and salt and beat to soft peaks. Add vanilla and beat to blend. Increase speed to high. Add sugar 2 tablespoons at a time and beat until stiff and shiny.

Spoon meringue into pastry bag fitted with plain ½-inch tip. Dab some meringue under corners of parchment to anchor paper to baking sheet. Starting in center of one traced circle, pipe meringue in spiral pattern to fill circle. Pipe 2 layers of meringue atop edge of circle to form sides. Repeat with remaining circles to form 6 meringues. Pipe any remaining meringue in short mounds on sheet to form meringue kisses (or cookies) if desired.

Bake until meringues are straw color and no longer sticky to touch, about 35 minutes. (Meringues will expand.) Turn off heat and let dry in closed oven 1 hour Cool completely at room temperature. *(Can be made 2 days ahead. Store airtight at room temperature.)*

FOR SAUCE: Stir plums, sugar, brandy and lemon peel in bowl to dissolve sugar. Let stand 30 minutes. *(Can be made 3 hours ahead. Cover and chill.)*

Place 3 small scoops of sorbet into each meringue. Spoon some plums and sauce over each and serve.

BALSAMIC BERRIES OVER VANILLA ICE CREAM

2 SERVINGS

CAN BE DOUBLED OR TRIPLED

½ 1-pint basket strawberries, sliced
1 tablespoon balsamic vinegar*
2 tablespoons sugar

2 tablespoons pine nuts
Pinch of ground cloves
Vanilla ice cream

Combine berries, vinegar and 1 tablespoon sugar in small bowl.

Combine remaining 1 tablespoon sugar, pine nuts and cloves in heavy small skillet. Stir over medium-low heat until sugar melts and pine nuts are golden brown, about 4 minutes. Transfer to plate if not using immediately.

Scoop vanilla ice cream into bowls. Top with strawberries, then with nuts.

Available at specialty foods stores and some supermarkets.

NOT GUILTY

EVER SINCE THE ARTIFICIAL SWEETener aspartame made its debut in 1981, it has been suspected of increasing one's appetite for sweet foods. But those suspicions are unfounded, according to an article by Dr. Barbara Rolls in the American Journal of Clinical Nutrition. After reviewing numerous studies of aspartame's effect on appetite, Rolls found that the sweetener does not promote excessive eating and that it may in fact help dieters avoid fattening foods. Rolls is director of the Laboratory for the Study of Human Ingestive Behavior at Johns Hopkins School of Medicine.

Lemon Ice Torte with Strawberry-Rhubarb Sauce

This simple-to-prepare recipe makes more sauce than you'll need for the torte. Use the remainder as a breakfast fruit, topped with a dollop of plain yogurt, or to accompany hot matzo meal pancakes.

8 SERVINGS

CRUST

3 cups blanched slivered almonds, toasted (about 12 ounces)
½ cup sugar
5 tablespoons margarine, melted
¼ teaspoon ground cinnamon
⅓ cup strawberry preserves
3 pints lemon or pineapple ice, sherbet or sorbet

SAUCE

1 cup sugar
½ cup water
1 vanilla bean, split lengthwise
1 20-ounce bag frozen unsweetened rhubarb
1 20-ounce bag frozen unsweetened strawberries
1 1-pint basket fresh strawberries
Fresh mint sprigs

FOR CRUST: Combine almonds and sugar in processor and chop finely. Transfer to medium bowl. Combine margarine and cinnamon and mix into almonds. Transfer to 9-inch-diameter springform pan. Using plastic wrap as aid, press almond mixture firmly 2 inches up sides and then over bottom of pan. Freeze 15 minutes.

Preheat oven to 350°F. Place pan with crust on cookie sheet and bake 20 minutes. If crust sides slip, press back in place with back of fork. Transfer pan to rack and cool crust completely.

Melt strawberry preserves in heavy small saucepan. Pour into cooled crust and spread to cover bottom. Cool. Soften ice very slightly and spread in pan. Freeze until firm. (*Can be prepared 1 day ahead. Cover and freeze.*)

FOR SAUCE: Combine ½ cup sugar and ½ cup water in heavy medium saucepan. Scrape in seeds from vanilla bean; add pod. Simmer 5 minutes. Add remaining ½ cup sugar and stir to dissolve. Add rhubarb. Bring to boil, reduce heat, cover and simmer until rhubarb is tender, about 8 minutes. Add frozen strawberries and bring to simmer Cool. Cover and refrigerate until well chilled. (*Can be prepared 1 day ahead.*)

Remove vanilla pod from sauce Cut between crust and pan sides with small sharp knife. Remove pan sides. Spoon ½ cup sauce over center of torte. Mound fresh strawberries in center. Garnish with fresh mint sprigs. Cut torte into slices and serve with sauce.

TRIO OF SORBETS WITH RASPBERRY COULIS

Refreshing in looks and taste, these light fruit sorbets served in a colorful raspberry sauce (below) are perfect after a filling meal. There will be leftovers of each sorbet to enjoy later.

8 SERVINGS

BANANA SORBET

1½ pounds ripe bananas (about 4 medium-large)
⅔ cup sugar
½ cup water
2 egg yolks
1 tablespoon plus 1 teaspoon fresh lemon juice
Pinch of salt
Pinch of ground ginger

APRICOT SORBET

2 cups water
1 cup sugar
1 6-ounce package dried apricots
½ cup dry white wine
⅛ teaspoon ground ginger
Pinch of salt

KIWI SORBET

1 cup sugar
½ cup water
2 pounds kiwis (about 9 large), peeled, diced

Raspberry Coulis (see recipe)
Fresh banana slices, kiwi slices and raspberries (optional)

FOR BANANA SORBET: Place bananas in freezer to chill 10 minutes. Bring sugar and ½ cup water to simmer in heavy small saucepan over medium heat, stirring until sugar dissolves. Beat egg yolks in small bowl to blend. Gradually whisk hot syrup into yolks. Return mixture to same saucepan and stir over low heat just until bubbles appear at pan edge and mixture thickens slightly, stirring constantly, about 2 minutes. Pour yolk mixture into processor. Add fresh lemon juice, salt and ground ginger. Peel cold bananas and slice. Add to processor bowl. Puree until smooth. Immediately transfer custard to ice cream maker and freeze according to manufacturer's instructions. Transfer to container and freeze. (*Sorbet can be prepared 2 days ahead. Store in freezer.*)

FOR APRICOT SORBET: Bring 1 cup water and 1 cup sugar to boil in heavy small saucepan over medium heat, stirring until sugar dissolves. Pour into processor bowl and cool.

Combine remaining 1 cup water, apricots and wine in heavy medium saucepan. Cover and cook over medium-low heat until apricots are very tender, stirring occasionally, about 25 minutes. Add mixture to syrup in processor. Add ginger and salt and puree. Cool.

Transfer apricot mixture to ice cream maker and freeze according to manufacturer's instructions. Transfer sorbet to container and freeze. (*Can be prepared 2 days ahead. Store in freezer.*)

FOR KIWI SORBET: Bring sugar and ½ cup water to boil in heavy small saucepan over medium heat, stirring until sugar dissolves. Cool.

Puree diced kiwi in processor Set aside 1 cup puree. Strain remaining puree through fine sieve Combine both purees and syrup in ice cream maker and freeze according to manufacturer's instructions. Transfer to container and freeze. (*Sorbet can be prepared 2 days ahead. Store in freezer.*)

Spread Raspberry Coulis in center of each dessert plate Arrange 1 scoop of each sorbet on sauce Garnish with fresh fruit if desired and serve

1½ cups sugar
1½ cups water

RASPBERRY COULIS

MAKES ABOUT 2⅔ CUPS

2 12-ounce bags frozen unsweetened raspberries, thawed
½ cup sugar
¼ cup raspberry jam

Puree all ingredients in processor Strain through fine sieve. (*Can be prepared 2 days ahead. Cover and refrigerate.*)

FROZEN BOYSENBERRY SORBET AND CHOCOLATE ICE CREAM BOMBE

An impressive do-ahead dessert. This is one that works well with thawed frozen unsweetened berries, too, so save the recipe to use after berry season.

10 SERVINGS

BOMBE

4 cups fresh boysenberries or blackberries or frozen unsweetened, thawed

2 pints chocolate ice cream, softened slightly
4 ounces semisweet chocolate, finely chopped

BOYSENBERRY SAUCE

3 cups fresh boysenberries or blackberries or frozen unsweetened, thawed, lightly crushed
⅔ cup sugar
2 tablespoons blackberry-flavored brandy (optional)

Additional berries
Fresh mint sprigs

FOR BOMBE: Overlap 2 sheets of foil in 10-cup metal bowl, leaving 2-inch-overhang. Press foil so it adheres to bowl. Place bowl in freezer. Puree berries in processor. Strain through sieve set over large bowl, pressing on solids with back of spoon. Bring sugar and water to boil in heavy large saucepan over medium-

high heat, stirring to dissolve sugar. Boil syrup 2 minutes. Mix syrup into berry puree. Refrigerate until well chilled.

Transfer berry mixture to ice cream maker and freeze according to manufacturer's instructions. Spoon sorbet into prepared bowl. Using back of spoon, spread sorbet over bottom and up sides of mold, forming 1¼-inch-thick layer and leaving well in center. Freeze until firm, about 3 hours.

Transfer chocolate ice cream to medium bowl. Mix in chopped chocolate. Spoon ice cream into center of bombe; smooth top. Freeze until firm, about 4 hours. (*Can be prepared 3 days ahead. Cover with foil; keep frozen.*)

FOR SAUCE: Combine 3 cups berries, sugar and brandy, if desired, in heavy large nonaluminum saucepan. Bring to boil, stirring frequently. Reduce heat and simmer 3 minutes. Cover and refrigerate until well chilled. (*Sauce can be prepared 2 days ahead.*)

Peel top piece of foil off bombe. Turn bombe out onto platter; peel off foil. Sprinkle fresh berries atop bombe and onto platter. Garnish with mint sprigs. Let stand 10 minutes. Cut bombe into wedges. Serve with sauce

BEST OF BOTH WORLDS

EACH OF THE 150 TEMPTING RECIPES in *Lean or Lavish* by Judith Pacht (Warner Books, 1991) has two exciting versions to choose from—one for when you need to count calories and another for when a little indulgence is in order. Nutritional data follow each recipe to help you weigh your options. Tips on menu planning are included, and wine suggestions from Hank Rubin, longtime wine columnist for *Bon Appétit*, round out the book.

POACHED NECTARINES WITH HAZELNUT ICE CREAM AND RASPBERRY SAUCE

4 SERVINGS

ICE CREAM

½ cup hazelnuts
3 cups whipping cream
1 cup half-and-half
6 egg yolks
⅔ cup sugar
¼ cup Frangelico (hazelnut liqueur)

NECTARINES

3 cups Riesling wine
¾ cup sugar
1 cinnamon stick
4 firm ripe nectarines, quartered, pitted
1 10-ounce package frozen sweetened raspberries, thawed

Fresh raspberries
Fresh mint leaves

FOR ICE CREAM: Preheat oven to 375°F. Place hazelnuts on cookie sheet. Roast hazelnuts until skins begin to blister, about 15 minutes. Wrap hot hazelnuts in kitchen towel and rub to loosen skins. Cool completely. Finely grind hazelnuts in processor Transfer ground nuts to bowl and set aside.

Bring 2 cups whipping cream and 1 cup half-and-half to simmer in heavy medium saucepan. Whisk 6 egg yolks and sugar in medium bowl to blend. Gradually whisk in hot cream mixture Return mixture to saucepan and stir over medium-low heat until custard thickens and leaves path on back of spoon when finger is drawn across, about 3 minutes; do not boil. Strain mixture into large bowl. Mix in ground hazelnuts, Frangelico liqueur and remaining 1 cup whipping cream. Cover and refrigerate hazelnut mixture until well chilled.

Transfer hazelnut mixture to ice cream maker and process according to manufacturer's instructions. Freeze in covered container. (*Ice cream can be prepared up to 1 week ahead.*)

FOR NECTARINES: Bring Riesling wine, sugar and cinnamon stick to boil in heavy medium saucepan, stirring frequently until sugar dissolves. Reduce heat, add nectarines and simmer until just tender, about 15 minutes. Cover and refrigerate nectarines in poaching liquid until well chilled, about 4 hours. (*Can be prepared 1 day ahead.*)

Puree frozen raspberries in processor. Strain to remove seeds. Cover and refrigerate raspberry sauce until well chilled, about 2 hours. (*Sauce can be prepared 1 day ahead.*)

Scoop hazelnut ice cream into bowls. Drain nectarine segments and discard poaching liquid. Spoon nectarine segments over hazelnut ice cream.

Drizzle with raspberry sauce. Garnish with fresh raspberries and fresh mint leaves and serve

Cookies

When all you want is "a little something," a crisp, freshly baked cookie fills the bill just right. Satisfy your taste for something sweet with Nutmeg Hearts, Easy Vanilla Wafers, Lemon-Anise Pirouettes or Chocolate Mint Melt-Aways—or any of the other easily prepared, quickly baked treats that follow. Add a cup of coffee or tea, and you'll leave the table feeling perfectly satisfied.

Molasses Spice Leaves

These Christmas cookies are topped with white icing and silver dragées for added elegance. Look for the dragées in the cake decorating section of your supermarket.

MAKES ABOUT 48

COOKIES

½ cup walnuts (about 2 ounces)
2 cups all-purpose flour
¼ cup sugar
½ cup (1 stick) unsalted butter, room temperature
½ cup firmly packed golden brown sugar
2 teaspoons vanilla extract
¼ cup unsulfured molasses
1 egg
½ teaspoon ground cardamom
½ teaspoon ground ginger
½ teaspoon ground allspice
½ teaspoon ground cinnamon
½ teaspoon baking soda

ICING

3 cups powdered sugar
2 large egg whites
Silver dragées

FOR COOKIES: Finely grind walnuts in processor. Add ¼ cup flour and ¼ cup sugar and blend to powder. Using electric mixer, cream butter with brown sugar and vanilla in large bowl until fluffy. Beat in molasses and egg. Mix remaining 1¾ cups flour with nut mixture, spices and baking soda. Stir into butter mixture (dough will be soft). Divide dough into 2 pieces. Flatten each into disk. Wrap each disk tightly in plastic and refrigerate 1 hour.

Preheat oven to 350°F. Butter heavy large cookie sheets. On heavily floured surface, roll 1 dough piece out (keep remainder refrigerated) to thickness of ⅛ to ¼ inch. Cut out cookies using 3-inch leaf cookie cutter. Transfer to prepared cookie sheets, spacing ½ inch apart. Repeat rolling and cutting with second dough piece. Gather scraps and chill 15 minutes. Reroll scraps and cut out more cookies. Bake until golden, about 10 minutes. Cool on racks.

FOR ICING: Using electric mixer, beat sugar and egg whites until smooth.

Spoon icing into pastry bag fitted with 1/16-inch round tip. Pipe icing atop cookies. Decorate with dragées. Let stand until icing sets. (*Can be prepared 2 weeks ahead. Store refrigerated between layers of waxed paper in airtight container. Let stand 5 minutes at room temperature before serving.*)

CRANBERRY AND RASPBERRY STAR COOKIES

Perfect for the holiday season. Cranberries add tang to the filling of these colorful sandwich cookies. You will have some small unsandwiched cookies, too.

MAKES ABOUT 36
SANDWICH COOKIES

COOKIES

¾ cup (1½ sticks) unsalted butter, room temperature
1 teaspoon vanilla extract
¼ teaspoon grated lemon peel
1 cup sugar
1 large egg
1 egg yolk
2¼ cups all-purpose flour
¼ cup cornstarch
¼ teaspoon (generous) ground cloves

FILLING

1 cup fresh cranberries
¼ cup sugar
¾ cup raspberry preserves
Powdered sugar

FOR COOKIES: Using electric mixer, cream butter, vanilla and lemon in bowl until light. Gradually add sugar and beat until blended. Beat in egg and yolk. Combine flour, cornstarch and cloves. Beat half of dry ingredients into butter mixture. Stir in remaining dry ingredients. Gather dough into ball (dough will be soft). Divide dough into 4 pieces; flatten each into disk. Wrap each in plastic and chill 1 hour.

Preheat oven to 350°F. Butter heavy large nonstick cookie sheets. Roll 1 dough piece out (keep remainder refrigerated) on floured surface to thickness of ⅛ inch. Cut out star-shaped cookies using floured 3-inch star cutter. Transfer to prepared cookie sheets, spacing ½ inch apart. Repeat rolling and cutting with second dough piece. Gather scraps and reroll, chilling dough briefly if soft.

Cut out more 3-inch star cookies. Transfer to prepared cookie sheets. Chill cookies 10 minutes. Bake until edges are golden, about 10 minutes. Cool on rack.

Roll third dough piece out on lightly floured surface to thickness of ⅛ inch. Cut out star-shaped cookies using floured 3-inch star cutter. Cut smaller star out of center of each 3-inch star using 1¾- to 2-inch star cutter. Transfer star outlines to prepared cookie sheets using floured metal spatula as aid. Repeat rolling and cutting star outlines with fourth dough piece. Gather scraps and star centers and reroll, chilling dough briefly if soft. Cut out 3-inch stars. Cut smaller stars out of each 3-inch star. Transfer star outlines and centers to prepared cookie sheets. Chill cookies 10 minutes. Bake until edges are golden, about 9 minutes. Transfer cookies to rack and cool.

FOR FILLING: Finely chop cranberries with sugar in processor. Transfer mixture to heavy medium saucepan. Mix in preserves. Cook over medium-high heat until mixture is reduced to scant 1 cup, stirring occasionally, about 8 minutes. Pour into bowl and cool.

Using metal icing spatula, spread 1 teaspoon jam filling in center of each 3-inch cookie, spreading slightly toward points of star. Lightly sift powdered sugar over star outlines. Place star outlines sugar side up over jam-topped cookies. *(Can be prepared ahead. Place in single layers in airtight containers. Refrigerate up to 4 days or freeze up to 2 weeks. Let stand 10 minutes at room temperature before serving.)*

LEMON HAZELNUT SQUARES

MAKES 16

CRUST

1 cup all-purpose flour
1/4 cup sugar
1/4 teaspoon salt

6 tablespoons (3/4 stick) chilled unsalted butter, cut into pieces
1/4 cup chopped husked toasted hazelnuts

FILLING

3/4 cup sugar
2 eggs
3 tablespoons fresh lemon juice
1 tablespoon minced lemon zest
1/2 teaspoon baking powder
Pinch of salt

Powdered sugar

FOR CRUST: Preheat oven to 350°F. Line 8-inch square baking pan with foil; butter foil. Mix flour, sugar and salt in processor. Add butter and nuts and blend until fine meal forms. Press onto bottom of prepared pan. Bake until light brown around edges, about 18 minutes.

MEANWHILE, PREPARE FILLING: Blend first 6 ingredients in processor.

Pour filling onto hot crust. Bake until filling edges begin to brown and

is just springy to touch, about 20 minutes. Cool completely in pan on rack.

Lift foil and dessert from pan. Gently peel foil from edges. Cut dessert into 16 squares. *(Can be prepared 1 day ahead. Wrap tightly; chill.)* Sift powdered sugar over squares; serve at room temperature.

EASY VANILLA WAFERS

To give these cookies a pretty curved shape, drape them over a wooden dowel or the handle of a wooden spoon immediately after removing them from the cookie sheet.

MAKES ABOUT 36 COOKIES

1/4 cup (1/2 stick) unsalted butter, room temperature
1/3 cup Vanilla Sugar (see recipe)
1/4 cup egg whites
1/3 cup unbleached all-purpose flour
Pinch of salt

Preheat oven to 400°F. Generously butter heavy large cookie sheets. Beat 1/4 cup butter and sugar in medium bowl until light and fluffy. Beat in egg whites. Gradually mix in flour and salt (batter will be soft). Drop batter by level teaspoonfuls onto prepared cookie sheets, spacing 3 inches apart. Bake until edges are golden brown and centers of cookies are still pale, about 7 minutes. Transfer cookies to racks and cool completely. (Can be prepared 1 day ahead. Store in airtight container.)

VANILLA SUGAR

Use this sugar to add a fresh-tasting vanilla flavor to all your favorite recipes. It's especially good when used to sweeten whipped cream.

MAKES 2 CUPS

2 cups sugar
1 vanilla bean, cut into small pieces

Process sugar and vanilla bean in processor until vanilla bean is very finely minced. Strain sugar to remove any large pieces of vanilla bean. Store sugar in airtight container

NUTMEG HEARTS

These look very pretty when presented on a plate of sliced strawberries.

MAKES ABOUT 16

1 frozen puff pastry sheet
  (½ 17¼-ounce package), thawed
2 tablespoons sugar
½ teaspoon ground nutmeg

Preheat oven to 350°F. Roll pastry out on lightly floured surface to 11x14-inch rectangle. Using 3- to 4-inch heart-shaped cookie cutter, cut out hearts. Transfer to cookie sheet. Combine sugar and nutmeg in bowl. Sprinkle over hearts. Bake until cookies are puffed and golden brown, about 15 minutes. Transfer to rack and cool. (Can be made 1 day ahead. Store airtight.)

LEMON-ANISE PIROUETTES

Enjoy the crisp, delicate treats on their own or with ice cream or mousse.

MAKES ABOUT 60

½ cup sugar
¼ cup powdered sugar
2 teaspoons grated lemon peel
1 teaspoon aniseed, finely chopped
½ teaspoon fennel seeds, finely chopped
6 tablespoons (¾ stick) unsalted butter, room temperature
3 large egg whites, room temperature
½ teaspoon vanilla extract
½ cup all-purpose flour

Position rack in center of oven and preheat to 350°F. Lightly butter large nonstick cookie sheet. Blend first 5 ingredients in processor 1 minute. Using electric mixer, cream butter in medium bowl until light. Gradually beat in sugar mixture, egg whites and vanilla. Add flour and beat until combined.

Drop 1 teaspoon batter onto prepared cookie sheet. Using back of spoon, spread into 3-inch round. Repeat 5 more times, spacing cookies evenly. Bake until cookies are golden brown on edges, about 5 minutes.

Immediately run tip of small knife under edge of 1 cookie. Using fingertips, pick up cookie at lifted edge and turn over onto work surface. Working quickly, roll cookie around handle of wooden spoon, pressing cookie against handle as you roll. Slide cookie off handle. Repeat rolling with remaining cookies on sheet, returning sheet briefly to oven if cookies begin to harden.

Rinse cookie sheet under cold water. Dry with towel. Lightly butter cookie sheet. Repeat making cookies with remaining batter in batches, rinsing, drying and buttering sheet between each batch. Cool cookies. (*Can be prepared 2 weeks ahead. Transfer to airtight container; store at room temperature.*)

RASPBERRY GALETTES

Crisp anise cookies are layered with raspberries and honey-flavored cream. There are enough cookies to make four desserts, with extras for nibbling.

4 SERVINGS

COOKIES

1⅓ cups unbleached all-purpose flour
¾ cup plus 1 tablespoon powdered sugar
¾ teaspoon aniseed, chopped
Pinch of salt
½ cup (1 stick) unsalted butter, room temperature
1 large egg yolk
1 tablespoon vanilla extract
1 egg, beaten to blend

SAUCE

2 cups (about 8 ounces) frozen whole unsweetened raspberries, thawed
3 tablespoons honey, preferably orange or other fruit flavor

FILLING

1 cup crème fraîche* or whipping cream
3 tablespoons honey, preferably orange flavored
2 ½-pint baskets raspberries or 1 1-pint basket strawberries, sliced
Powdered sugar
Fresh mint leaves

FOR COOKIES: Combine flour, sugar, aniseed and salt in bowl of heavy-duty mixer fitted with paddle attachment. Add butter, yolk and vanilla and mix at low speed until coarse meal forms. Knead dough into smooth ball. Flatten to disk, wrap in plastic and refrigerate 40 minutes.

Preheat oven to 350°F. Roll dough out on lightly floured surface to scant ⅛-inch thickness. Using 3½-inch fluted cutter, cut dough into rounds. Transfer rounds to heavy large cookie sheets, spacing evenly. Gather dough scraps. Repeat rolling and cutting until all dough is used, chilling dough briefly if soft. Brush cookies with beaten egg. Bake until light golden, about 12 minutes. Transfer cookies to rack to cool. (Can be prepared 3 days ahead. Store cookies in airtight container.)

FOR SAUCE: Puree raspberries and honey in blender. Strain. (Can be prepared 2 days ahead. Cover and refrigerate.)

FOR FILLING: Beat crème fraîche and honey in chilled medium bowl until stiff peaks form. Transfer filling to pastry bag fitted with ⅜-inch (no. 3) star tip.

Place 1 cookie on flat surface. Pipe filling in small stars over cookie. Place 1 layer of raspberries atop stars. Top with second cookie. Pipe filling in small stars over second cookie. Place layer of raspberries atop stars. Top with third cookie. Sift powdered sugar over. Place 1 raspberry in center. Repeat layering of cookies, filling and berries to make

3 more desserts. Spoon sauce onto plates. Transfer 1 galette to center of each plate. Garnish with mint leaves and serve.

*Available at specialty foods stores and some supermarkets.

CHOCOLATE MINT MELT-AWAYS

Festive piped cookies spread with minted white chocolate and coated with dark chocolate. Great for after dinner.

MAKES ABOUT 42

COOKIES

1 cup (2 sticks) unsalted butter, room temperature

2 teaspoons vanilla extract

½ teaspoon peppermint extract

½ cup plus 2 tablespoons powdered sugar

2 cups all-purpose flour

GANACHE

¼ cup plus 2 tablespoons whipping cream

2 tablespoons (¼ stick) unsalted butter

9 ounces imported white chocolate (such as Lindt), chopped

¼ teaspoon peppermint extract

COATING

9 ounces bittersweet (not unsweetened) or semisweet chocolate, chopped

1 tablespoon solid vegetable shortening

FOR COOKIES: Preheat oven to 350°F. Butter 2 heavy large cookie sheets. Using electric mixer, cream butter and extracts in medium bowl until light. Beat in sugar. Beat in half of flour. Stir in remaining flour. Spoon half of dough into pastry bag fitted with no. 4 star tip. Pipe 2½-inch-long ovals with solid centers on prepared cookie sheet, spacing cookies ½ inch apart. Repeat with remaining dough. Bake until golden brown on edges, about 12 minutes. Transfer to paper towels and cool.

FOR GANACHE: Bring cream and butter to simmer in heavy small saucepan over low heat. Add chocolate and stir until smooth. Mix in extract. Refrigerate just until firm enough to spread, stirring occasionally, about 30 minutes.

Line 2 cookie sheets with foil. Using small metal icing spatula, spread 1 teaspoon ganache over flat side of 1 cookie. Arrange ganache side up on prepared cookie sheet. Repeat with remaining cookies. Refrigerate until ganache is firm, about 30 minutes.

FOR COATING: Melt bittersweet chocolate and vegetable shortening in top of double boiler over simmering water, stirring occasionally until smooth. Remove from over water.

Dip 1 end of 1 cookie into bittersweet chocolate. Grasp cookie on sides and dip ganache side into bittersweet chocolate; shake cookie to remove excess chocolate. Place cookie on same sheet, chocolate side down. Repeat with remaining cookies. Chill until chocolate sets, 30 minutes. Remove cookies from foil. *(Can be prepared 2 weeks ahead. Refrigerate in single layers in airtight containers. Let stand 10 minutes at room temperature before serving.)*

GUILT-FREE DESSERTS

SPRINGY PINWHEELS WITH RASPBERRY jam, dense brownies layered with toasted nuts, swirled double-chocolate cheesecakes—not exactly hearthealthy desserts, are they? But believe it or not, you'll find them among the 150 low-cholesterol recipes in *Sin-Free Desserts* (Doubleday, 1991) by Jean Anderson. The innovative creations may sound decadent, but they go light on traditional ingredients, such as butter, eggs and heavy cream, and have been created with an eye on fat and calorie counts to boot. Available in bookstores everywhere.

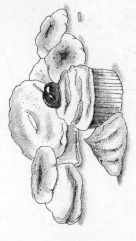

MOCHA-HAZELNUT MACAROON DOMES

If you're short on time, you can skip the white chocolate decoration.

MAKES ABOUT 30

MACAROONS

½ cup hazelnuts, lightly toasted (about 2½ ounces)
½ cup sugar
1 tablespoon all-purpose flour
1 large egg white
1 teaspoon vanilla extract

MOCHA GANACHE

¼ cup plus 2 tablespoons whipping cream
3 tablespoons unsalted butter
1 teaspoon instant coffee granules
9 ounces imported milk chocolate (such as Lindt), chopped
1 teaspoon vanilla extract

COATING

9 ounces bittersweet (not unsweetened) or semisweet chocolate, chopped
1 tablespoon solid vegetable shortening
30 (about) small raspberries or hazelnuts
3 ounces imported white chocolate (such as Lindt), chopped

FOR MACAROONS: Preheat oven to 350°F. Line 1 large cookie sheet with parchment. Brush lightly with vegetable oil. Finely grind hazelnuts in processor. Add sugar and flour; blend to powder. With machine running, add egg white and vanilla; blend to paste.

Spoon mixture into pastry bag fitted with no. 4 (⅜-inch-diameter) round tip. Pipe ¾- to 1-inch-diameter mound onto parchment about ½ inch high and spacing 1 inch apart. Dip finger into water

and gently press top of cookie to flatten center slightly. Bake until golden brown, about 12 minutes (cookies will spread to about 1½ inches). Turn parchment (cookies will adhere) over onto work surface. Brush parchment with just enough water to moisten. Let stand until parchment can easily be pulled off cookies, about 2 minutes. Peel off parchment.

FOR GANACHE: Bring cream and butter to simmer in heavy medium saucepan over medium heat. Add instant coffee granules; stir to dissolve. Reduce heat to low. Add chocolate; stir until melted. Mix in vanilla. Pour into bowl. Chill until firm enough to spread, stirring occasionally, about 45 minutes.

Line cookie sheet with foil. Using icing spatula, spread 1 heaping teaspoon ganache onto flat side of each cookie, mounding to dome in center. Place ganache side up on prepared cookie sheet. Repeat with remaining cookies. Chill until ganache sets, 20 minutes.

All the Right Tools

In addition to a selection of baking pans (which might include a baking dish, bread pan, cake pan, cookie sheets, pie pan, custard cups or ramekins, soufflé dish, spring-form pan and tart pan), you will need a few essential tools to get the job (of baking) done right. Before buying, though, consider the kind of cooking you do: Are pies your weakness, cookies your specialty? Also, be sure to figure in the size and dimensions of your oven, the availability of storage space in your kitchen and your budget. As with most anything, it's worth investing in quality: Well-made tools will last a long, long time; cheap ones often self-destruct just when you need them most.

FOR COATING: Line cookie sheet with aluminum foil. Melt bittersweet chocolate with vegetable shortening in top of double boiler over simmering water, stirring until smooth. Remove from over water. Grasp 1 cookie between thumb and index finger. Dip ganache portion into melted chocolate. Shake off excess. Turn chocolate side up and place on foil-lined cookie sheet. Top with raspberry or hazelnut. Repeat with remaining cookies. Refrigerate until chocolate sets, about 30 minutes.

Melt white chocolate in top of double boiler over simmering water, stirring until smooth. Dip spoon into chocolate. Wave from side to side over cookies, forming decorative pattern. Refrigerate until white chocolate sets, about 15 minutes. Place cookies in single layer in airtight containers; chill overnight. (*Can be prepared 3 days ahead.*) Let stand 10 minutes at room temperature before serving.

Light Desserts

In the effort to maintain a wholesome diet, many people feel that they "blow it" on desserts. But ending a meal with a deliciously satisfying treat doesn't have to mean loading up on fat and calories. Instead, capitalize on dishes made with fruit, or try some of the many lowfat, no-cholesterol desserts now on the market. And, if you must, remember that moderation is the key. So just have a small slice of that marble fudge cheesecake.

Ripe fresh fruit—either puréed or diced—is a healthy replacement for fudge or butterscotch sauces.

If you have a recipe for a molded dessert or trifle that calls for pound cake, substitute angel food cake, which is lower in calories, fat and cholesterol.

In a muffin, coffee cake or chocolate cake recipe specifying sour cream, try yogurt as a healthful substitute.

Baste baked apples with apple cider for a simple, naturally sweet dessert.

A sophisticated and easy-to-prepare low-calorie dessert: peaches or pears poached in sweet wine, such as late harvest Riesling or Muscat.

Use sorbet or sherbet instead of ice cream for à la mode desserts.

Serve cookies that are made with egg whites, such as macaroons and meringues, instead of butter-rich treats.

Good-for-You Cookbooks

LOW FAT & LOVING IT by Ruth Spear (Warner Books, 1991). According to the author, the key to cutting back on dietary fat while still enjoying the foods you love is to reduce rather than eliminate your intake of rich ingredients, including cream, butter and eggs. She shows you just how to do this in two hundred recipes ranging from the traditional (apple pancakes and firehouse chili) to the exotic (Philippine grilled pork tenderloin).

THE ART OF LOW CALORIE COOKING by Sally Schneider (Stewart, Tabori & Chang, 1990). The tempting recipes and lovely photographs in this volume are designed to help all diet watchers eat deliciously, elegantly and with style.

BEYOND CHOLESTEROL by Peter O. Kwiterovich, Jr., M.D. (The Johns Hopkins University Press, 1989). In this comprehensive book on heart health, authoritative, detailed explanations clarify everything you ever needed to know about high cholesterol and related conditions. The recipes prove you don't have to suffer if you're on a low-cholesterol diet.

SKINNY SPICES by Erica Levy Klein (Surrey Books, 1990). Liven up your cooking with any of the 50 recipes here for homemade spice blends. Choose from hot and spicy, sweet, herb and ethnic combinations—all low in fat, calories and sodium. Mail-order sources for many herbs and spices are also included.

INDEX

ACKNOWLEDGEMENTS & CREDITS

Recipes supplied by:

Melanie Barnard
James and Sidney Bonnet
Anne Boulard
Michael Chiabaudo
Russell Cronkhite
Jane Davis
Brooke Dojny
Jim Fobel

Gary Goldberg
Harris Golden
Mr and Mrs. Laurent Hamon
Martin Johner
Karen A. Kaplan
Kristine Kidd
Elinor Klivans
Jan Liascos

Lori McKean
Perla Meyers
Donna Chrisco Oldford
Betty Rosbottom
Richard Sax
Mary Sellen
Gina Schild
Ilana Sharlin

Edena Sheldon
Marie Simmons
Dede Spaith
Hubert Surville
Tarla Thiel

Concept:
Susan M. Allyn

Graphic design:
Sandy Douglas

Production:
Joan Valentine

Proofreader:
Katie Goldman

Editorial development and original writing:
Norman Kolpas

Illustrations:
Sharon Holm

Index:
Barbara Wurf

Rights and permissions:
Gaylen Ducker Grody
Susan Mills